Be

Spiritual

Love Age Needs You

Tommy Knestrick

Be Spiritual
Love Age Needs You

Copyright © 2011 by Tommy Knestrick

Writing and drawings by Tommy Knestrick
Edited by Loretta Medenciy
Cover by Rob Knestrick
Graphic art by Andrew Knestrick

For information about special discounts or bulk purchases, please contact www.TommyKnestrick.com.

The author of this book does not dispense medical advice or prescribe the use of any technique as a form of treatment for physical, emotional, or medical problems without the advice of a physician. The author's intent is only to provide general information to help you in your quest for social and spiritual well-being. If you use the information in this book, which is your right, the author and the publisher assume no responsibility for your actions.

ISBN 13: 978-0615551319 10: 0615551319

Love Age Press
P. O. Box 292987
Sacramento, California 95829
Printed in the United States of America

DEDICATION

To my wife and spiritual partner, Audrey, who is partly responsible for helping me being spiritual.

To my four children, Rob, BJ, Scott, and Kim and my four grandchildren Darrell, Jenn, Andrew, and Sean. I am so thankful the Divine helped place them in my life to give the lessons and help I needed for learning to be spiritual.

To those with the courage and commitment to be spiritual during a difficult period in history when higher spiritual vibrations of love are needed to advance the Love Age.

Contents

In Gratitude

One of the attributes of being spiritual is to be grateful. When I thought about how this book became reality, I realized I had a lot to be grateful for.

Foremost, I'm thankful for my wife, Audrey who served as my spiritual partner along our life's journey, which had many difficult and happy times. She was a bright star of compassion that helped direct my heart toward the light of the Divine. Most of the time, she was aware that our old dogmatic spiritual paths had lost their usefulness and helped pull me along to higher levels. As a spiritual partner, she provided ample lessons that sparked my ego responses, which I had to learn to recognize and replace. She also served as an example of the love needed to help me mature spiritually. She was a significant part of the story that helped me co-create or be a spiritual being. My wish for you is that you have a spiritual partner to help you become more Spiritual as I did.

I'm grateful for our four children - Rob, BJ, Scott, and Kim that selected us, along with divine guidance, to be members of our family's lessons and experiences. They helped during my spiritual struggles to learn needed lessons and provide some of the lessons. We are a close nit family and they were not only subject matter for the book, but they also helped edit it. A note of information about pronouncing our last name, Knestrick. It is pronounced - nes·trick.

Usually on Sundays, we would meet and read a chapter, and they would provide needed editorial feedback. My grandchildren Jenn, Andrew, and Sean were often a part of the readings and provided valuable inputs that made the book better. Their valuable inputs surprised me at times. Some of the stories in the book were about my children and grandchildren, but at times, they requested some of them to be deleted. I want to give a special thanks to Rob who created the book's front and back cover and to his son, Andrew, for creating the graphic's art. I am grateful for my family and the help they gave me.

I am grateful for all the religions that were there when I needed them. The Methodist Church introduced me to the teachings of Jesus, the Quakers provided company for my non-violent beliefs and introduced me to directing my spiritual attention within, and Edgar Casey introduced me to the wisdom from within and reincarnation. Eckankar™ gave me the Eastern perspective of a direct relationship with the Divine. They all had a place in my spiritual development that helped make this book possible even though I am no longer associated with any of them.

I am grateful for the spiritual discussion group that met to discuss spiritual books in Marianna, Pennsylvania, my hometown. My sister Ruth Ann and her husband, Paul were members of it along with my cousin, Betty. Paul's mother Loretta and her two daughters, Bev and Monica were members too. They read copies of my chapters. I had been asking the Divine for someone who could edit my book other than my immediate family, and Loretta, a retired English teacher, from the Marianna book discussion group was provided.

Loretta would send back my chapters filled with comments and grammar corrections. I didn't realize how bad my book needed her input. When I finished the last chapter of the book, she asked me if I wanted her to go through the entire book again for consistency. I sure did. I am very grateful for her contribution to the book, and she along with the other members of the discussion group are in my eyes, pioneers of the Love Age.

I am grateful to Don A. Singletary who helped with information about self-publishing, which helped me get this book ready for publication. I am also thankful for CreateSpace, a POD publisher, which is under the umbrella of Amazon. Com. They are truly a blessing for those who want to self-publish.

I am thankful to all the authors, comedians, and scientist that have provided information used in this book. No book stands alone since knowledge is an accumulation of information and wisdom from the past and present. There are always those in the past that have provided insights and wisdom that have brought us now to a major shift in consciousness of spirituality. Spirituality has been around for thousands of years and there isn't much new except more and more people experiencing higher levels of it and finding new ways to help others experience it. I am grateful for these spiritual people and their wisdom.

Most importantly, I am grateful for the Divine's help I received. When I started to write this book about being spiritual with the Divine as my partner, I was actually not allowing the Divine to be my writing partner. Gradually, I was given lessons along the way about being a co-creative writer and the need to collaborate with the Divine. These lessons opened up an inner connection with the Divine where I eventually could access its wisdom. I am so thankful for the lessons that allowed me to have a more direct connection with the Divine and I hope it has made it a better book for you to become spiritual.

The term ECKANKAR is a trademark of ECKANKAR P.O. Box 27300, Minneapolis, MN 55427 U. S. A.

Introduction

I recently saw the documentary film, *I Am* created and directed by Tom Shadyac, but do not confuse it with the movie, *I Am* with the same name. Tom was the Hollywood director of *Liar Liar, The Nutty Professor, Bruce Almighty,* and other movies. After he had a life threatening accident, he started questioning his Hollywood style of living and gave it up to live in a trailer park where he also started to seek answers to important questions about life.

In the film, *I Am,* he interviewed scientists, thinkers, and people who were interested in implementing paradigm shifts to change the world from conflict to cooperation. He asked two questions and the first one was. *What is wrong with our world?* Shadyac's final answer for this question was - I AM.

This was the same answer I had for this question except I was a little more specific about the "I AM." It's the ego self and its consciousness of conflict, fears, greed, unconscious reactions, unhappiness, intolerance, attachments, and doing what's good-for-me.

Be Spiritual

Tom Shadyac's second question was - *What can we do about it?* Again, his basic answer was "I AM." We are responsible to make personal life changes in small steps that will eventually help change the world.

I too addressed the question of what can we do about the world to make it a better place as well as to stop the trend toward world conflict, unhappiness, and its possible destruction. My answer was to *be spiritual*. By being peaceful, cooperative, loving, joyful, free, consciously choosing intentions, and using good-for-all motivations, we not only change our personal lives for the better, but it also affects the rest of the world. By changing yourself, you change the world. It is that simple.

This book discusses five major shifts in consciousness I took to transition to a more loving self and to affect the world for the greater good. To start with, I had to make a shift from identifying myself as the ego self to the Divine Self. Secondly, I had to change the way the ego self separates itself from others, nature, and the Divine to a consciousness where I realized I was interrelated with the same spiritual consciousness as the Divine that is in all things. Also, the ego consciousness of desiring and doing what is good-for-me was in need of shifting to a consciousness where the good-for-All thrived. The fourth shift was a personal spiritual transformation from ego-empowerments to spiritual-realizations. Finally, the personal and collective changes from all of the above shifts combined to move me out of the Ego Age consciousness to the Love Age. These, plus a few other shifts, which will be discussed in another book are what makes you more spiritual.

All of these shifts in consciousness have to happen first within us. This is why it is so important for you to be spiritual. If you change your ego consciousness, you also change the world's ego institutions by means of the interconnected energy webs that create chain reactions of broader physical, social, and ecological changes. Quantum scientists are aware of how all matter and its energies inter-connect throughout multiple layers of interacting systems. This is why shifting into the Love Age requires changing yourself first rather than trying to change others. So, what's right with the world? It is to be *SPIRITUAL* – a divine being filled with divine wisdom, power, and love automatically helping to change the rest of the world for the greater good.

Is being spiritual your purpose??

When I originally thought about writing this book, I just wanted to share experiences of how I learned to co-create with love. After reading other authors and observing what was going on in the world, I realized that my own experiences were part of a larger shift in consciousness. I then decided to integrate my personal experiences into what others saw as an evolutionary leap into what I call the Age of Love. However, this shift is not a sure thing since it depends on enough people consciously choosing to change their own consciousness. If you make this commitment, you can be a spiritual pioneer of the Love Age and help usher it in.

Would you like to live directly connected with the Divine where you can receive inner wisdom and love to fill your being with peace, freedom, joy, love, purpose, and wisdom? Would you like to have the Divine as a co-creative partner directly working with you for your good as well as others? Would you like to contribute to a major shift in the evolution of awareness where peace, love, tolerance, and a higher wisdom fill hearts with good-for-All intentions and actions? Is 2012 a possible end or a spiritual shift? Would you like to know what the Divine wants for your life's purpose? Would you like to be spiritual? If your answer is yes to some of these questions, this book is for you.

Have you had an experience where a subtle nudge from within gave you inner wisdom to resolve a difficulty? If you have, even if it was unrealized at the time, this was a spiritual experience with your divine partner guiding and empowering your life with love and wisdom. Spirituality initiates loving intentions, which allows your divine partner to guide you through difficulties to find spiritual solutions. Your divine partner is present 24/7 to help you receive what you want to be, to do, or to have.

***

This all-knowing partner helped me continue writing this book at a time when I seriously thought about giving up. After about seven years of writing, I threw out my original manuscript, restructured the book many times, and edited chapters more times, than a porcupine has quills. I had actually rewritten one chapter 209 times. Unfortunately, the book still read like a lifeless, sterile technical report that was painfully similar to the ones I wrote as a doctoral candidate at the University of Pittsburgh or as a professor at Westminster College. With a mindset of academic rationality and being dyslexic, it was difficult to write and especially from the heart.

I wondered, would I ever learn to write so love would flow from the book's pages? At one point in writing this book I asked myself, why not stop trying to write and enjoy my retirement? To my surprise, what started out as a highly negative and frustrating writing experience eventually helped me learn more about using divine guidance to receive a deeper understanding of how to express myself with love.

One day while writing, I felt frustrated. I decided to move from my desk to the recliner where I meditated. I wanted to bring my emotions back into balance to feel inner calmness and receive guidance. After a few minutes, a subtle telepathic impression gently settled into my consciousness, "Go to the bookstore to find a book on how to write."

That's all I received. What kind of guidance was that? Was the message for real or just a stray thought running through my mind? I had learned from previous

4

experiences that if I didn't listen to my inner feelings and messages, I would live to regret it. I thought, what harm would it be if I went to the local bookstore? Besides, I would like to take a walk to get away from this depressing study.

While looking through the books at the bookstore, the title, *If You Want to Write,* by Brenda Ueland caught my attention. It was the subtitle, *A Book about Art, Independence and Spirit* that really perked my interest. What did she have to say about spirit and writing, I wondered?

When I looked through the first few pages and saw when it was published, I wondered how a book originally published in 1938, the year I was born, would be of help in today's publishing environment? I then turned to the back cover and read, "... her best-selling classic on the process of writing that has already inspired thousands to find their own creative center." Since I wanted to find my creative center, I continued reading. It said, "she writes with love and enthusiasm, in a direct, simple, passionate and true way." That's exactly how I want to write, I thought.

As I read these words, I became aware of a Beatles' song playing on the bookstore's audio system. It was *"All You Need Is Love."* I thought, there goes that song again. It served to give me two other messages from the Divine, and each time it helped clarify questions about incorporating love into my life and book. Was this another message of guidance, I wondered?

I thought either this song was directing me to buy the book, or the source of my inner guidance was a die-hard Beatles' fan. I just knew it was a personal message from the Divine and decided to buy the book.

Once I arrived home, I was anxious to read it. I knew from experience that messages from the Divine always had my well-being at heart, and I was learning more and more to trust them. I had many of these experiences before, and I am still amazed how they arrived unexpectedly and at the exact time I needed them. This was what Carl Jung, the psychologist, meant by synchronicity and it is how the relationship with the Divine sometimes works. This is an example of one of the ways the Divine can directly communicate from within to bring miracles that touch our daily lives.

***

I was deeply influenced by what Ueland's book had to say about writing from her creative center where words and ideas flowed from within. I felt this would probably help me learn to use and trust my own inner source of divine wisdom for writing.

The creative center Ueland spoke about was a source I had known, but I hadn't used it for writing since I felt more comfortable using my rational mind. Unfortunately, it restricted the inner flow of love like leaves clogging a roof's gutter. I had to clear out the rational leaves from my mind's gutters and trust the thoughts, feelings, and love flowing from within. If I did, love and wisdom would flow into the book's pages. It was ironic that I was writing about the importance of trusting inner source of guidance, but I wasn't completely opening my heart at that point to use its guidance while writing.

Eventually, I realized another important aspect about writing. In the beginning, I thought all I had to do was to write about love, when I should have been *writing with love*. This inner writing voice of love was how I wanted my pages to resonate.

I've always found that it's easier to learn lessons from my own or others' life experiences than when someone tried to tell me something. When I'm told something, I might learn a little. When I have an experience or read about someone's experiences, they are easier to understand and to remember the spiritual principles. I will therefore share as many of my experiences as possible to help you understand spirituality. They will include some of the irrational things I've done as well as some of my more successful experiences. For me, a mental picture of an experience is worth billions of words, and I hope sharing them helps you understand how spirituality can work in your own daily life.

I went through many trial-and-error experiences to learn to be spiritual. The five shifts evolved mainly from my own personal experiences of hard knocks and pain. It has been said, a wise person learns from his or her mistakes as well as from others. I'm sure you'll see your own life experiences in some of mine, hopefully the better ones. It is my hope that by sharing the lessons I learned, it helps you reach the goal of being spiritual faster and with less pain and struggle than I did.

While this book is based on my personal spiritual development of learning to be spiritual, it isn't a chronological listing of significant events or turning points from birth to now. Instead, the five shifts provide the structure for the book's contents.

There are seven primary reasons why I wrote this book. I hope they open your heart to love and help you learn a way of living with divine guidance, peace, joy, and harmony as well as for the good of the world.

The primary purpose was to *help you be spiritual* in order to ignite higher energy vibrations for making your everyday life more of what you want it to be. This spiritual power consciously uses your divine gifts of freedom of choice, soul awareness, good-for-all intentions, divine wisdom, and love. They help tame the ego consciousness by placing Soul in charge of your thoughts, feelings, visualizations, and more. I have used this spiritual power to change ego habits, careers, buy homes, lose weight, and to be a more spiritual and loving being.

The second purpose was to use *scientific or evidence-based information wherever possible to help explain and vali-*

date spiritual principles. I have had a career in the social sciences where I conducted research and taught sociology. I have also spent over 40 years using firsthand observations of my spiritual experiences and communications with the Divine to learn how to co-create with love. Spirituality is similar to science in that it relies on firsthand observations for knowing rather than relying only on secondhand sources of faith-based dogma, rituals, and myths as religions do. Basing my life on firsthand observations and experiences was very important in helping me to be spiritual.

Science and spirituality are increasingly complementing each other rather than in a perpetual state of conflict like ego-based science and faith-based religions are. We are approaching a threshold of a new age of wisdom where science and spirituality will continue to complement each other especially at the quantum levels. As much as possible, I want the book to be evidence-based; but I don't want the book to read like a dull academic report.

Using humor to enliven the book and your life was the third purpose. Humor helps bring joy, and joy helps create love. Humor is, therefore, a valuable spiritual tool when used for these purposes rather than for criticizing, being intolerant, or vulgar. Humor makes us smile and laugh, which scientists know releases endorphins that improve physical and emotional health.

Some of my family did not like some of my humor, so I'm sticking my neck out hoping you the reader will like at least a little of it. Bear with me since we all do not like the same kind of humor, but I am hoping as you read the book I can occasionally squeeze out a few of your endorphins.

Too often, religious people believe they should be serious, unemotional, and humorless to be spiritual. I believe H. L. Mencken said, God was a comedian speaking to an audience that was afraid to laugh. The Divine loves humor and I want to use it whenever I can to help put joy into life.

The fourth purpose was to *enrich your life with love*. I've learned that life is so much better when I'm living it with love. I now have the tools to turn difficult situations into spiritual solutions where the Divine guides me to do what is good-for-All. Life has more peace, joy, freedom, and purpose now. This is what I, as well as the Divine, want for you.

Do you want it too?

This book will allow you to *compare your experiences and desires with mine to make the book more of an experience rather than something you just read*. To facilitate this fifth purpose, I have asked questions within the text and at the end of chapters about your experiences or commitments to help make you pause, to initiate conscious awareness, and to help you relate it to your life. The questions at the end of chapters can also help facilitators of book discussion groups to get members to be more aware of their own life experiences. A life where the ego is recognized is one that you can consciously change.

The sixth purpose was to help you *recognize ego's unconscious fear-based reactions and to replace them with love-based habits or solutions*. This is ego-realization while the replacement of ego habits relies on Soul-realization and co-realization. The ego consciousness of the mind is fear and conflict-based, and it has created a serious social crisis making life polarized and an unhappy affair. Once there is a realization of unproductive ego habits, they can be replaced with spiritual ones. The Age of Love depends on transitioning from the negative consciousness of the Ego Age.

The seventh purpose was *to help you realize that the world has a greater probability of becoming more spiritual if your relationships and actions shine with love*. When you change, the world changes too. The Love Age arrives by a spiritual person doing one or more small loving action each day. This is how important you are for your own life's happiness and the improved consciousness of the world.

***

Mary had just gotten off the school bus after a half day attending her kindergarten class. Her mother saw tears in her eyes as she stepped off the bus. "Mary, what's wrong? Why are you crying?"

"Johnny told me his father said the end of time is coming and there will be a lot of deaths. If there is no time, I'll not know when to wake up, eat, or go to the school bus. What will happen to my Cinderella watch? He also said the world will be destroyed and I'm afraid to die."

Mary's mother wiped the tears from her eyes as they walked home. "Mary, you don't have to worry about time going away or the world being destroyed. There are some people that believe that, but your dad and I don't. In fact, if people like you and I choose it, the world will be a much happier, loving, and peaceful place to live. Wouldn't that be nice?"

"Oh yes. Does that mean I can keep my Cinderella watch?"

***

What do you believe about the end of time? Some recently believed it was to happen on May 21, 2011 but it didn't, while others believe it will happen in 2012. Are humans or natural disasters going to destroy Earth or are we going to change our consciousness to bring love and harmony into personal and collective relationships? I believe the latter has a higher probability of occurring, and a significant evolutionary change in consciousness is already happening. However, the likelihood of it happening increases when you accept the spiritual way of love.

Since we all have the freedom of choice, the Age of Love will not happen automatically. Do you want to be part of an evolutionary change of awareness that is shifting from an ego consciousness to spiritual enlightenment that will help bring peace and love to our planet? During the process of writing this book, I learned that this was my life's purpose. I hope it will be yours too.

What is your life's purpose?

When I started writing this book, I only wanted to share it with members of my former religion. After writing for some years, I began to realize that the book should be written for a worldwide audience. I began to realize there was a major evolutionary change in consciousness happening, and it dealt with the spiritual principles I was writing about. Instead of wanting to share my experiences with just my former religion, I wanted to help contribute to the shift in consciousness for the Love Age.

The Love Age needs no churches, central leaders, or membership fees. It relies on you alone changing your own ego habits and living with love-based relationships in your personal life. Meeting in small groups can help form small communities of love where you can experience help in transforming yourselves to be a spiritual pioneer for the Love Age.

If you want to be a part of this, do not only read this book but also put it into practice. The U. S. Army once had a slogan –"An Army of One." You instead can be a "Spiritual pioneer of One." One person at a time will co-create the Age of Love by changing their ego consciousness into living a life of divine love. The world desperately needs you. That is how important you are for the evolution of your own life's consciousness and that of the world.

Being religious or non-religious doesn't matter. If you have problems with words like God, Spirit, or other religious words, please substitute Universe, Universal Wisdom, Universal Source or Force, Energy, or other words acceptable to you. Words are only pointers to something, not the real thing, so don't allow a reaction to words stop you from reading or accepting spiritual principles. I use Divine Source or

11

Divine to refer to God while different religions use other names.

Being spiritual is not the same as being religious. People on an institutionalized religious' path who submit to the authority of their religion and have blind faith in its dogmas, rituals, myths, worship services, sacred books, and leaders are not being spiritual. If a person has a partnership and a direct relationship with the Divine's love and wisdom, they are spiritual. Many of the mystical branches of religions have this relationship. However, being a member of a practicing religion does not exclude one from being spiritual. They would instead have to be less influenced by institutional practices and live a more direct and personal relationship with the Divine.

The fastest growing spiritual group in America is those who do not belong to a religion and simply identify themselves as spiritual. Those who were raised by parents that were not religious like mine have become increasingly disillusioned with the secular life. They don't like religious organizations, but feel more comfortable with being spiritual. I currently do not belong to any established religion and prefer to call myself spiritual. Spirituality requires an open and loving heart and if that is what you have or want, this book is for you.

Are you willing to take one small step to be more spiritual to become a pioneer of the Love Age?

SHIFT I

Ego Self to a Divine Self

Who am I? Humans have been seeking an answer to this question for ages. Most people believe themselves to be the body/ego self, which consists of the body and aspects of the mind, subconscious mind, social culture, and emotions that make up the ego. This is what people refer to when using the words "I" or "me." Families, religions, science, and other social institutions strongly influence how you define the ego self, while spiritual people experience a different concept of who they are. Humans are divine beings and this is the self that needs to be placed in charge of the ego. In order for the Love Age to evolve, the consciousness of the world must transition from the ego identity to the Divine Self. The world is in need of this paradigm shift. This is the only way individuals and societies can consciously infuse divine love, wisdom, and spiritual solutions into their lives and the world. This was a shift I had to make to be spiritual.

Chapter One

Paradigm Shift to a Divine Self

Mary's father was waiting in his car to pick her up at kindergarten. It was a rainy day and Mary was dressed in a pink raincoat with a matching umbrella. He noticed she was trying to tiptoe around water puddles. When she eventually reached the car, he buckled her in the child's seat as quickly as he could. He noticed she was frowning. "What's wrong honey? Is the strap too tight?"

"No Daddy. I just don't want to be a shoe any more. They get too dirty and wet."

"What do you mean you don't want to be a shoe?"

"You're the one who told me, I'm a shoe."

"When did I say you were a shoe?"

"Didn't you tell me to say, 'I'm Sole?' I don't want to be the bottom of a shoe anymore."

***

15

Most people are as confused as Mary about who they are. Those who cannot see beyond the body and ego self will often react like Mary by diminishing the self's identity to something physical or mental. I lived that illusion for 35 years or more before I realized the ego wasn't my true self. The Divine Self or Soul was the true self and should be in charge of the ego self.

We are faced with the choice of continuing with the ego's destructive ways, which could include the demise of humans as a species as well as other life forms. The alternative is to realize we're divine beings capable of creating love and harmony in personal and social relationships.

We need to transition into a more cooperative, peaceful, and loving consciousness or realize our worst destiny. In order for you to be spiritual, an identity paradigm shift must be made. Instead of the ego, the Divine Self and its love and wisdom should be guiding your intentions and actions.

The ego's negative values and habits must cease to control the Divine Self and assume a supportive status. The ego's unproductive reactions and habits need to be recognized, taken responsibility for, and replaced. These are the 3-Rs for initiating and placing the Divine Self in charge. *Recognize it* (ego habit). *Responsible for it*. *Replace it*. This shift in consciousness is needed in order to initiate the spiritual habits of love, peace, joy, and freedom.

Do We Have More than One Self?

Before I attended church as a teenager, I thought I only had one self. After becoming familiar with the concept of soul as a Christian, I became aware that I might be more than one self. While on Earth, it seemed I had a soul floating around in Heaven, and when I died, I would become it. I understood I was the ego self while living on Earth and would become soul once I passed on.

16

When I read about early Quakers, they practiced silent group meditations to experience the profound peace of the "Inner Light." It was my first introduction to going within to find the presence of the Divine Self.

While I was a Quaker, I tried out Transcendental Meditation, since it proclaimed itself as a way to find inner peace. I didn't remain in the group very long since the meditation wasn't effective. In addition, I was told I had a personal mantra, but the same mantra was given to other followers too.

In the late 1960s, I made a discovery that shattered the illusion of only being an ego self with a soul in Heaven. During this time, my wife was also exploring spiritual frontiers and she introduced me to Edgar Cayce. Cayce would go within to channel medical and other spiritual wisdom, and I wanted to be able to tap into that source of inner wisdom too.

Cayce also helped me accept reincarnation. According to reincarnation, I had two selves - a divine soul and an earthly ego self. The earthly physical or ego self was temporary for a given life until the body died, but the real self, Soul, was eternal and reincarnated life after life in new bodies. I also learned karma derived from past life ego motivations and actions and were carried with me life after life until I learned their lessons of love.

After Cayce, my next introduction to Soul was in Eckankar™ where I learned I was Soul now and could use it to travel into inner spiritual dimensions. I didn't have to wait till I died to experience Soul or the spiritual worlds since I could project there now. I learned I was already my Divine Self, my true identity. I was also not limited to an earthly self that existed only as physical and mental forms. In addition, I was Soul now with spiritual awareness and powers. I was a divine being or Soul, and it was this higher self that should be in charge of the ego self. I'm still working on placing Soul in total charge.

We Are Fraternal Twins with an Ego Self & a Divine Self

The Divine, Soul, and Subtle Energy Fields

To understand who we are as Soul, it is necessary to know the relationship between the body/ego self, subtle energy fields, Soul, and the Divine. Soul (Divine Self) is the bridge for Divine Energy to enter the body, mental, and emotional energy fields. When I use the word "Divine," I am referring to the Divine Self as well as the Divine Source and Divine Energy. The Divine is a trinity.

Figure 1.1 represents the three as Divine Source, Divine Energy, and Divine Self that serve to channel divine love, wisdom, and co-creative energy into subtle energy bodies, physical body, and creates life as well as maintains it. The Divine is within and surrounds you and is everywhere. It is not an upper external layer as depicted in the illustration. The picture uses earthly space and time, but in reality, there is no up or down, one location, beginning or ending, or space and time when it comes to the Divine Source, Divine Energy, or Divine Self.

The hearts flowing from the Divine Source with sparkling halos represent divine love. When you are a clear channel for this love, it affects thoughts, memories, emotions, physical body, physical environment, and social life. When the ego does not block the divine flow, the Divine Self is energized to co-create with love.

Divine Source

Figure 1.1 serves to show how divine love flows into your life when the Divine Self is in control as opposed to the ego self. The word, Divine Source is usually referred to as God

Figure 1.1

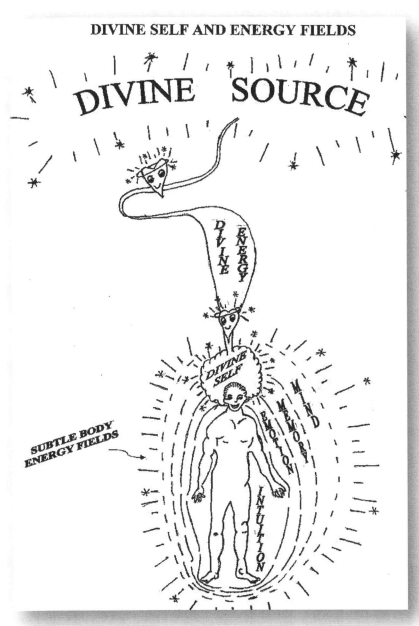

by most religions. The Divine Source is also called the Unmanifested, One, All, Allah, Jehovah, Brahma, and other names.

These are only symbolic names pointing to the real thing. Since religions have used God to justify violence, distributor of wrath, and other unloving acts, this word carries a lot of negative baggage. I therefore prefer to use a more neutral word. The name is not what is important since it is only a word pointing to the real Divine. What is most important is experiencing the Divine rather than its name. Even children have their own idea about God's name.

**

Johnny and Chris were arguing about the name of God during recess. Johnny said, "His name is Harold."

Chris said, "No-sir, His name is Andy! Where did you ever get the name Harold?"

"When we pray the Lord's Prayer, don't we say? 'Our father in heaven. Harold be your name ....' See, Harold's his name."

"You're not saying it right. Besides, in the song, 'He Walks with Me' that we sing in church, we sing, 'An-dy walks with me; An-dy talks with me ...' See his name is Andy."

This joke requires some understanding of Christian practices. For example, the Lord's Prayer is supposed to read, "Our father in heaven. *Hallowed* be your name..." The song, "He Walks with Me," is supposed to have the lyrics, "*And he* walks with me; *And he* talks with me..." Does this help?

**

The Divine has no him or her gender. I use the pronoun "*It*" most of the time when referring to the Divine Source. This is about the best pronoun available in the English language to refer to something without giving it a gender bias. Our language is so ego biased toward gender identity that it does not have a pronoun to refer to neutral gender beings that exist in spiritual forms or dimensions.

The Divine Source is the foundation from where all love, wisdom, life, unmanifested energy and all else derives to manifest forms in the material and spiritual worlds. It's the source of all unmanifested energy, which becomes manifested forms. Unmanifested creative energy at the subatomic level is what makes all things in the universe exist. When affected by divine consciousness or the thoughts of humans, it manifests as forms that we see in the outer world.

Divine Energy

Divine Energy flows from the Divine Source and carries all of the divine goodies like love and wisdom with it. Religions refer to the Divine Energy as Holy Spirit, Life Force, *Chi, Reiki,* spirit, to name a few. Quantum scientist who theorize string theory refer to it as "strings." The essence of divine love, wisdom, and co-creative energy derive from the Divine Source in the form of Divine Energy. These inner divine attributes flow through Soul as a passageway to enter the subtle energy fields, body, and material world. Divine Energy is what you experience as love, divine wisdom, light, sound, and co-creative energy. It is in every atom of the spiritual and material worlds of form.

As the Divine Energy moves from the Divine Source into the world of matter, its vibrations progressively become lower. The first reduction of Divine Energy from unmanifested energy is observed in the form of sound and light vibrations. This is why those who have Near Death Experiences or experience divine presence usually see lights, light beings, and hear the sounds of the spiritual worlds.

Divine Self

21

You and I are Divine Energy individualized as the Divine Self or Soul, which makes us divine beings of energy. Divine Self has the power of awareness by which it can observe what is going on in spiritual dimensions, subtle energy bodies (mental and emotional), physical body, physical world, and social environments.

Since the Divine Self evolved from Divine Energy, it is embodied with divine love, wisdom, and co-creative energy. Divine Self has the power to direct attention and connect us with the energies of love and wisdom to co-create matter and circumstance with the Divine as a partner. The Divine Self also has the power of co-creating for the good-for-All when it works in harmony with the Divine. It can consciously use thoughts, emotions, and imagination to help co-create the world of matter out of the unmanifested energy that flows from the Divine Source. The Divine Self can guide its intentions with divine wisdom and co-create for the good-for-All.

The Divine Self Dwells within Me as the True Me

This Divine Self is our true identity. It is eternal and never dies as the ego body does. This eternal identity carries past life choices and their consequences from one life to another and is stored within the subtle bodies. This karma is what determines much of our experiences and circumstances in life and provides the lessons we need to learn.

When there is no ego barrier blocking spirit; love, wisdom, divine guidance, and co-creative powers will freely flow into you. This places Soul in charge as a benevolent being producing peace, freedom, justice, love, and joy in relationships. Without the Divine Self in charge, the ego remains in control and you suffer the consequences of its unconscious and unproductive habits.

22

With Soul in Charge, Co-creating Is for the Good-of-All

I had to find ways to place Soul in charge by replacing ego habits with spiritual habits of love. Once the subconscious mind and emotions learned spiritual habits, it was easier for Soul to respond and live in harmony with the divine's purpose.

This was and still is one of the changes I'm consciously trying to fully implement. My desired relationship with the Divine is to have Soul in charge and to be the Divine's co-creative partner. This isn't the easiest task to do, which is why it is still a work in progress. Since life is a dance of balance between the inner and outer, the Divine Self must be the lead dancer to guide life's dance. This allows you to live in harmony with what's good-for-All.

Is Soul or the Divine the lead partner in your life's dance?

To summarize, the Divine Source is like the electrical power plant that produces the electricity (i.e., unmanifested energy, divine love, wisdom, co-creative energy, and life force). Divine Energy is the power lines that carry all of the essence or transmissions flowing from the electrical generating plant of the Divine Source to the world and us.

Electricity has to be reduced in power by transformers to be useful in homes, which is similar to the stepping down of Divine Energy to be useful in the inner worlds and our earthly existence. The Divine Self as well as our *chakras* that will be discussed in a later chapter serves a similar function as a transformer that lowers electricity to run refrigerators, dishwashers, and other useful electrical appliances.

Be Spiritual

Soul, thoughts, feelings, and imagination help convert unmanifested energy into manifested energy for useful purposes when it is in a co-creative relationship with the Divine and others. Divine Self serves as a channel to allow the life force or energy (Divine Energy) to manifest life, animate and maintain the body, and other biological, social, and spiritual functions.

Unfortunately, the ego is like a terrorist destroying the electrical power lines that transmit wisdom and love that could flow into Soul and eventually into our homes of the self. When this happens, disharmony, unhappiness, and other ego consequences happen until you realize its destructive presence. You need to be the electrical worker that goes out during an ego storm and recognizes ego's unconscious reactions in order to reconnects your home to the power lines of love and wisdom flowing into and from the Divine Self. This is what a spiritual person does.

For you to be spiritual, you must shift your identity from the ego self to the Divine Self. It will make your personal relationships more loving and peaceful. In the next chapter, the ego terrorist will be examined as the enemy within.

Figure 1.2

SUGGESTED QUESTIONS FOR PERSONAL AND GROUP DISCUSSION

1. How do you answer the question, "Who am I?"
2. Do you now view your true self as Soul or the Divine Self?
3. How do you create the things you want in your life?
4. What pronoun do you use to refer to the Divine (e.g., he, she, it, mother/father, etc.)?
5. Do you view the relationships between the body, energy fields, and Divine differently than depicted in Figure 1.1?
6. Do you believe your true self is the Divine Self or Soul?
7. Have you experienced the divine love and wisdom of Divine Energy?
8. Have you experienced the inner light or sound of Divine Energy?
9. Have you experienced Soul being the conscious observer of your ego habits?

☺ *Smile* ☺
You're true self is not the ego.
You're a divine being with spiritual powers

Chapter Two

Ego is the Enemy Within

If you asked yourself the question "who am I," most would identify with their body, mind, emotions, and how their cultural values, beliefs and roles define them. These are the elements of the ego self or what some may refer to as the "I." It is the primary way humans' identify themselves and distinguish themselves from others.

Egos are unconscious mental constructions derived mainly from social institutions. The ego is not a solid piece of reality that exists or stands alone by itself. Instead, it is mainly a mental illusion that is socially constructed and maintained by the family, education, government, economy, and religion of the society we are born and live in. The family is a powerful determiner of the ego consciousness since it often determines our national, cultural, religious, political party, economic class, and educational opportunities. The family to a great extent defines the ego's identity since it determines whether we our religious or secular. For example, the secondary status of women in Moslem cultures is to a great extent determined by their religion.

Some people do not accept the ego definitions their society defines for them. A spiritual person is one who does not accept the ego consciousness of his or her society. Individually, we have the freedom to choose what we want to be and choose our own identity. Todays' youth are doing this more and more frequently than past generations, and the women's movement is also gaining more worldwide influence.

Ego identity is a Mentally Constructed Illusion of Society

As a teenager, the church constructed my faith-based ego, and I wasn't aware it was being done. I decided to attend church on my own because I felt an inner emptiness with my parent's lack of religion. For some reason, I thought attending church would eliminate this empty feeling.

I accepted most of the church's beliefs on faith especially the Bible being the infallible word of God. Since the Bible was the record of God's communication, I strongly believed it to be true and rejected anything suggesting otherwise. Either I had faith in it or I didn't. It was a black or white issue with no middle ground for questioning the interpretation of the Bible I was given. Conforming to my religion's interpretation of the Bible built my ego's faith-based self.

***

When I later attended West Virginia Wesleyan College to be a Methodist minister, I attended a New Testament Bible class taught by Dr. Teeple. He was a biblical scholar who had researched the Bible in its original text. He valued evidence-based knowledge above church dogma and was an impressive scholar. Fortunate for me, he presented a different interpretation of the Bible compared to what I believed. He was familiar with how the Bible changed over time to agree with the beliefs of those in charge of cultural values. The Bible actually incorporated the ego cultural beliefs of its time, such as subjecting women to a second-class citizenship. This was not what Jesus taught nor practiced since women were included as part of the early Christian leader-ship. Dr. Teeple taught me that the Bible was not the infallible word of God as I thought it was.

I learned the New Testament was written 60 to 100 years after Christ's death and was based on secondhand stories passed from one person to another before it was written. Can you imag-ine what would happen to the story of your life if we waited 60 to 100 years after your death to record it? The professor also told us that the spiritually inspired writers of the New Testament's four gospels were affected by the culture of their times and used dif-ferent sources to compile their accounts of Jesus' life. The gospel writers of Matthew and Luke used the gospel of Mark and a "Q" source. In addition, the Bible had gone through various transla-tions and interpretations where passages were changed to agree with later cultural or religious beliefs. This was all in direct con-flict with what I believed, and I refused to believe what he was teaching about the Bible. My ego-based faith in the Bible was being challenged, and my ego reacted to protect itself like others in my class.

During a college event where students could invite par-ents to attend classes, some of the students brought family members to the New Testament class. One of the students who believed as I did decided to criticize the professor for teaching lies about the Bible. She probably gained the courage to say what she did since her parents were present.

She said, "The Bible is the written word of God and not written by men. If you teach such a thing, you'll go to Hell."

Her attack had emotionally shaken the professor. He did his best to dispute her deeply hurting ego reaction. I felt sorry for him. He was an honest, gentle, truthful, and good man from what limited perceptions I picked up from classroom contact. I knew he was deeply concerned about his students and bent over backwards to help us understand his truth about the Bible. I didn't think it was fair for the student to say what she did, even though I agreed with her blind-faith in the Bible. My reactions to protect the ego were kept internal, unlike her scathing vocal condemnation of the professor.

I listened to the professor during the rest of the semester and much of what he said made sense, but I still didn't want to step outside my faith in the Bible. My blind-faith and ego attachments to what the church taught limited my freedom to choose or even consider new information based on objective observations. I reacted to any challenges to my faith-based ego, but it softened over time.

Being confused for almost two years, I went back and forth in my beliefs, until I eventually decided the professor was right. I stepped outside my blind-faith in the Bible and the fundamentalists' interpretation of Jesus' life. My belief in the Bible had been the basis of my religious faith and when that went, it opened doors to questioning other ego-base institutional beliefs. It also helped to redefine who I was and my beliefs.

Little did I know when I was a church member that I was taught an interpretation of Jesus life rather than Jesus actual teachings. What I learned was mainly the dogma and myths that grew up around Jesus' life that were added to the Bible as well as being the church's interpretation of what Jesus taught. Scholars have concluded that it's difficult to know the historical Jesus.

Even the early Christian church had three major interpretations of Jesus' teachings. James viewed it as a part of Judaism; St. Paul's interpretation became the Orthodox Church that opened Christianity to gentiles; while the *Gnostics,* a more mystical group, were targeted for elimination by the Orthodox Church. Much of Christianity was a mental construction of the dogmas and myths of the orthodox group, which made it an ego-based institution as many religions are today.

It was the first time I realized social institutions helped construct my mental ego beliefs. I didn't think of it as being my ego at that time, but it was part of how I interpreted my identity of being a fundamental or evangelical Christian. Beliefs, dogmas, and myths of religion and other institutions were often the bars constructing my ego's prison. Recognizing my ego habits that derived from social institutions was the first step in helping me change them.

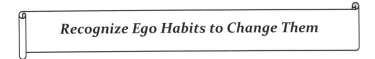

Recognize Ego Habits to Change Them

My New Testament professor was only at the college for two or three years. As I look back on this experience, I'm thankful the Divine brought him into my life to help move me to a higher understanding based on evidence, which helped serve as a guiding light for my spiritual quest.

The Divine often brought people into my life like the professor. Earlier, a student minister at my church encouraged me to attend Bethany College where he was attending. I planned to be a coal miner like my father, but the mines had laid off workers and were not hiring. I had to find something else to do.

I believed my minister was divinely placed in my life at that exact time to encourage me to attend Bethany College, which I was not academically prepared to do. The Divine was always using others to help me on my spiritual journey and guided me when my heart and spiritual eyes were not open enough to see where I should direct my life. These gentle encouragements from people and feelings of emptiness were often the way the Divine guided me early in my spiritual unfoldment. When I later realized how the Divine operated and guided me, I realized life was indeed purposeful.

***

Ego self is dogma-based while the Divine Self is evidence-based. During my sophomore year in college, I decided to major in sociology, which was a discipline based on scientific or evidence-based information about how society and groups affect behavior. Along with the New Testament class, it helped me

31

make the transition from a fundamentalist to liberal/social Christian as well as to make other changes in my life. The study of social institutions showed me how groups helped construct the ego consciousness via religious, political, educational, economic, and family values and beliefs through the process of socialization. I also thought sociology, based on scientific evidence, would help me know how to change institutions to make the world more peaceful and just. These academic influences helped transform my identity from a faith-based ego to rely more on evidence-based information.

I also became a believer in non-violence as a way to change society. I was disturbed with the Methodist and other churches for not realizing Jesus taught love and non-violence, which they chose to ignore. Instead, the church was justifying intolerance, injustices, and wars. I consequently decided to become a Quaker to focus my attention on the use of non-violence for changing governments of the world to be more peaceful and just. I didn't realize it at the time, but my personal life and societies collective ego consciousness were based on conflict, which was the major reason the world was a warring and violent place. I wanted to help reconstruct those mental ego beliefs of warring governments to transform them into instruments of peace.

Mind and Institutions Construct Ego's Reality

The Ego Is a Victim and Lives for the Good-for-me

When the ego consciousness rules life, it engages in good-for-me conflicts with others to maximize its selfish needs. It creates the hell-like circumstances that most people unconsciously live and is unfortunately the prevailing consciousness of humankind. It's what you see daily in your relationships with others and between nations.

Egos Are Always Me-deep into Themselves

The ego consciousness not only motivates the lives of individuals, but it also runs our ego-based institutions. When the ego consciousness runs social institutions, it also creates social disharmony, stress, greed, suffering, and unhappiness at the personal and community levels. *The ego self is greed and conflict-based.*

Have you noticed conflicts exist in most families, which creates family discord and can even lead to divorces? The conflicts and polarizations between political parties in the United States have made it very difficult for the country to make needed decisions to move us forward for the greater good. The greediness of Corporations and Wall Street serve the greedy rich and brought the economy to the brink of economic collapse, but they still resist reform. The educational system focuses mainly on the mind and is deeply imbedded in the ego consciousness of rationalism and dogmatic science. Religions fight with each other, among themselves, as well as with secular science and cultures. Religion is used to justify wars; practitioners will die for it and do anything except practice the love most religions teach. We are living in the Ego Age of increasing polarization and conflicts.

The ego consciousness has now arrived at an evolutionary end-point where conflict and disharmony are no longer serving *Homo sapiens.* Irrational thinking, intolerance, greed, and conflict control science and technology are creating wars as well as tons of misery and unhappiness.

33

Ego Is Addicted to Greed, Conflict, and Unhappiness

I believe it was Aldous Huxley who said that it just might be possible this world is another planet's hell. We may already be living the hell some had hoped to escape after death. William Sunday said, "If there is no Hell, a good many preachers are obtaining money under false pretenses." Maybe they are just not clear about where or what hell is. Could it be the ego consciousness within us?

Ego Complaining and Victim Consciousness

As a child, my parents were the primary influence of my beliefs and behaviors. Parents develop primary ego patterns for relating to us and to each other and pass it on to their children. My father was the one in control of family money and decisions. His main ego method of gaining control was to complain. My mother, on the other hand, responded with the victim consciousness of "poor me" and wanted her children's sympathy so we would side with her and be against my father. I primarily adopted my father's habit of complaining, but also used victim consciousness to control others too.

***

It wasn't until I was a freshman at West Virginia Wesleyan College that I began to become aware of how I used my mother's victim consciousness. When I met my friends on campus, they would often ask, "How are you doing?" This was a great opener for my victim consciousness to rise to its glory and tell them how bad my life was and hope they would feel sorry for poor me.

I noticed after a while they would try to avoid me, and I began to wonder why. When I exchanged greetings, I began to notice their negative reactions to my complaining about the

34

weather or the burden of being a student. I wanted them to feel sorry for me, but they didn't.

Later, after I realized I was using the same victim response my mother used, I no longer wanted to be a victim seeking sympathy from others. If I was going to change this ego habit, I had to recognize when I used it and to be aware of the disharmony it created. I gradually recognized how I used it to manipulate the sympathy of my fellow classmates and started to tone it down. Unfortunately, using the victim response was still a habit when I was later married but not as pervasive as my complaining. My wife and later my children would usually bring it to my attention when I unconsciously used the "poor me" victim consciousness.

In my relationship with my wife, I took on the complaining ego role especially when disagreements arose about finances while she in turn poured on the guilt. I was completely unaware that we had a complaining/guilt habit that made our ego's react and caused disharmony in the family.

It took me much longer to recognize the ego habit of complaining was also an extension of the "poor me" victim habit. Complainers view themselves as victims. I was in an ego prison and some of the bars were made out of complaints of being a poor victim of my wife's spending habits. Since I felt complaining gave me power and control, it took me some 50 years to recognize how its bars imprisoned me.

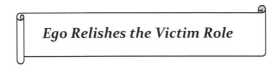

Ego Relishes the Victim Role

What main ego habit creates most of the bars of your ego prison?

35

***

How many egos does it take to screw in a light bulb? Actually, none. It is below their me-centeredness and over inflated ego superiority to do maintenance work. They would gladly sit in the dark complaining and arguing that someone else should change it. Such is the nature of the ego.

Recognizing the Complaining Ego

It took about 35 years of marriage before I became aware of the complaining/guilt relationship I had with my wife, Audrey. The ego response usually started with my projecting the next month's bills and realizing we would not have enough money or it was too close to call. This would create fears about our financial future, and I would start complaining to my wife.

"Just look at next month's budget, we're not going to have enough money and you're going to have to stop spending so much."

"I'm not the one who spends all the money. You're the one who bought the lawnmower this month."

"What did you expect me to do? I sure wasn't going to go out there and chew the grass off with my teeth. I had to buy the lawnmower. Besides, you said it was all right to buy it. You're the one who's buying clothes and other stuff all the time. Why don't you cut back on that?"

"If you had some wives, they would spend all your money."

"What do other wives have to do with next month's money? You should be doing something now to cut back on your spending. You're the cause of our budget problems."

"Probably when I die, you'll buy your next wife all the jewelry and clothes she wants and you'll not say a word to her."

Then the argument escalated into a shouting match and we would both be angry until it got so hot that one of us had to walk away. This ego reacting of back and forth complaints and guilt got us nowhere except to create disharmony in the family. I thought I won since I pointed out her bad spending habits, and she thought she won by making me feel guilty about mine. At times, I would feel bad not only because I felt angry that nothing was accomplished, but I felt guilty about the possibility of treating my imagined next wife better than I treated Audrey. Guilt is subtle, but it is also powerful.

Sometime around 1993 or 1994, we became aware of this unconscious ego habit and started to discuss it. Recognition of our unconscious ego habit was the first move toward changing it. When I started to look deeper into why this ego pattern started in the first place, I realized it was about my fear of financial insecurity of the future. I didn't like future uncertainties especially financial ones.

When I looked beneath any of my ego reactions, I discovered there was always some type of fear about loss associated with it. I was attached to a secure financial future and feared the possible loss of it. This then led to the irrational behavior of blaming my wife for our financial circumstances and complaining to try to control what I thought was her unwise buying. Did you notice the complainer is never at fault nor is the one using guilt? Each of us was protecting our ego identity by blaming the other one for our financial circumstances.

> ### *Threatened Ego Engages in Conflict to Protect Itself*

Audrey and I even went to the point of scheduling a short one-day trip to a lake in the mountains to discuss what we were going to do about this ego pattern of relating to each other. I took a pad and pen to record an agreement, which we called "The Manifest Proclamation of Freedom."

37

In the agreement, I was to try to catch my ego response of future financial problems before they turned into fears. If I didn't do this and began complaining, Audrey was to point out that I was complaining. I was to stop complaining and to discuss the situation without giving judgments or accusing her. If this did not work and Audrey started firing her guilt bullets, I was to bring it to her attention that she was using guilt. We hoped this would help each of us recognize how we were responding with ego reactions and stop the cycle of firing ego bullets back and forth at each other.

Well, I have to confess this approach did not work. If I caught my initial reaction of financial fear and stopped its reactions, it would usually work. If it went beyond that point where we had to remind the other spouse how their ego was reacting, we returned to our old ego pattern of escalating the argument. It seemed that when the other person pointed out what the ego was doing, the ego would feel threatened and reacted to protect itself. We would then fall back into our old reacting pattern of machine-gunning complaints and guilt to gain control over each other.

We gradually managed to gain some control over this problem when I decided to adopt my wife's attitude about money. She has a tremendous trust in the Divine that everything will be provided. So she keeps her focus on the present rather than the future like me. On the other hand, Audrey hates planning anything, especially finances, while I over plan. Life is a balance between trusting the Divine and doing what we need to do to make things happen. Some people over plan as I did and act without divine guidance or trust, while others rely too much on the Divine as though it was their free welfare system without any responsibilities. Audrey was not that far from the center or balanced state, but I had to give up my over planning and trust more in the Divine to stop the initial ego reaction before it escalated into a conflict.

For my part, I began to have more faith in receiving and trusting in the Divine by turning over the problem to it. Now, my wife does the finances, plans for the current month, and I wait for a financial disaster to happen. I hope you realize I'm just kidding about the last comment or am I?

The ego self devoid of love and trust in the Divine is the enemy within and this is the consciousness that we all need to change. Instead of operating my personal life with ego-based decisions and solutions, I had to replace them with love-based ones.

> ### *Ego or Intellect without Love Is the Enemy Within*

This was the first time I consciously recognized an ego pattern in my marriage and consciously did something about it. I learned that the ego and its negative reactions that caused disharmony was the true enemy within. Even though the ego is the enemy within, we are still responsible for loving it. Didn't Jesus say, "Love your enemies?" Hating the ego is reacting to it and it will continue to keep you in its grip. Loving and not reacting to it will free you.

Changing my attitude and behavior about financial insecurity helped minimize the ego's reactions, but I learned to never count fear out since it will raise its ego head when and where you least expect it. I had to keep vigilant of my reactions and the fears that caused them, which will be the topic of the next chapter and probably an issue I will have to address for the rest of my life.

Can *you name one ego habit that creates disharmony in your relationships?*

Figure 2.1

**SUGGESTED QUESTIONS FOR PERSONAL
AND GROUP DISCUSSION**

1. Is the ego consciousness responsible for creating the hell-like circumstances here on Earth?
2. How does your ego consciousness filter how you perceive reality?
3. Have you ever used the victim consciousness to get others to feel sorry for you?
4. What social institutions have you noticed using ego-based consciousness?
5. Have you ever tried stopping an ego pattern that you used when relating to others?
6. Have you ever tried to protect your ego from attack? If so, what reaction (anger, gossip, guilt, complaining, etc.) did you use?
7. Are you mostly unconscious or conscious of how the ego operates in your life?

☺ *Smile* ☺
The ego is the enemy within.
But aren't we supposed to love our enemies too?

Chapter Three

Ego is Fear-based

Meister Eckhart, a thirteenth century Catholic theologian, teacher, and mystic, believed that at the heart of one's spiritual life is the problem of attachment to things, people, beliefs, and other earthly things. He said, "To be full of things is to be empty of God. To be empty of things is to be full of God." At another time he said, "He who would be serene and pure needs but one thing, detachment."

Although Meister Eckhart did not use the word ego, the main function of the ego is to be attached to whatever it deems important for the good-of-me. If you are attached to things, there is a fear of losing them. *The ego is attachment-based.*

The way to rid yourself of a fear is to be detached from losing it. Since attachments are like mental glue, the way to dissolve the bond is not to place so much importance on things or circumstances. If you desire an automobile, good relationship, or success, accept and be grateful for what you already have, and do not let the worry or fear of not receiving it or its loss make you miserable. Hold a balanced emotion where you are neither overly joyful about having it or worried about its potential loss. Detach the mental glue.

> ## *Fears & Worries Are Paying High Interest on Something You Rarely Receive or Lose*

In Eastern religions, detachment is an important belief and practice. Detachment is easy to understand mentally, but it is difficult to practice. Since beliefs and status things define the ego, it does not want to give up these attachments. If I have lots of things, I'm a rich ego. If I lose my things, I'm a poor victimized ego. The bond between things and the identity of being rich is held together by ego's super glue.

Since the ego is built on mental attachments, the ego is ruled by the fear of losing them. Fears become powerful negative thoughts that energize emotions and direct life in irrational and conflicting ways. It is not a harmonious or peaceful way to live.

> ## *Fears Arise from Attachments*

My first step in changing an ego habit was to recognize it (e.g., my complaining), then to recognize its underlying fear that energized it (e.g., fear of the lack of money in the future), and finally to mentally detach from it. To help you recognize some of the underlying fears of the ego, I am going to list, explain, and give some examples. This is not an exhaustive list of fears.

Fear of Abandonment

The fear of abandonment is one of my wife's predominant fears. She lost her father when she was one and a half years old and her mother when she was in eighth grade. I feel certain that she had experiences of being abandoned in past lives since this fear seems to be one of her main lessons to learn in this lifetime.

42

Fear of abandonment is associated with the fear of being alone or the loss of loved ones.

When Audrey goes to the grocery store or shopping, she always wants someone to be with her. When we are in Minnesota during the summer time, she is lonely for her children and grandchildren in California. If I would die before her, she would most likely move in with our youngest daughter the next day or close to it.

Where there is fear of abandonment, it is difficult to trust those that are close to you. There is always an underlying fear that they will abandon you. Some have a haunting fear of losing someone in their family to an accident, illness, divorce, moving away from friends, or some other form of mini-death. This fear derives mainly from an attachment to people and the possible loss of them.

Fear of Losing Ego's Status

Since the ego constructs a social status or identity and is attached to it, there is always the fear of losing it. People are like actors since that rely on external popularity and acceptance but fear its loss. Teens are threatened with the fear of not being accepted by their peers. They are vulnerable to this fear since they are trying to become more independent of parents and at the same time develop stronger ties with their peers. They will often dress in strange ways or do things to be like their peers that are different from what their parents want them to be or do.

In addition, there is the fear of losing one's sense of self-worth, which is a very fragile thing since the ego tries to define it using external approval. Your worth is outside yourself like the popularity of movie stars and is difficult to control. Social achievements are short lived, which makes self-worth vulnerable. There is also the fear of embarrassment that can put dents into one's ego.

Fear of Losing the Body or Physical Appearance

The fear of one's own death is one of the major fears in our culture. Since the ego places so much emphasis on the body rather than the Divine Self that continues to exist after death, its loss is a frightening thing. Some religions make their members worry about going to Hell. When they get close to life's end, the ego does not like the thought of possibly going to Hell or ending up being nothing but dust in a grave.

There are fears associated with the loss of the ideal social images how the body should look. The thoughts of becoming old and no longer looking like a young beautiful woman or handsome man are prevalent fears. This is especially true for those who have relied on their appearance as the main ego way for evaluating their self-worth. There are those that fear gaining weight and some of them become anorexic and carryout extreme measures to lose it.

Fear Loss of Power

Power and control over others as opposed to love is a central value of the ego consciousness. Since the ego operates for the good-of-me, it wants to control circumstances and people to get what it wants. Have you noticed the people at work, churches, social groups, and the family who have a strong attachment to being the boss or the one in control? They also have the fear of losing their power and strike out to defend it when necessary.

My wife's guilt and my complaining were ways of struggling for control in the family. Our egos reacted with strong emotions to try to defend what we thought was our piece of the family power.

Power Conflicts Make for Unhappy Relationships

Terrorist know that if they can put fear into the enemy, they can control them. Fear is a means of controlling others. Political parties use the fear of terrorist, communism, socialism, taking your guns, loosing Medicare, and many other fearful things to get votes and gain control.

When I was a fundamentalist Christian, they used the fear of Hell as a means of control. I concluded that there was no Hell and if there was Conrad said, "The belief in a supernatural source of evil is not necessary; men are quite capable of every wickedness."

When I was in Eckankar™, they told its members that if they left the religion, they would have serious karmic difficulties and lose their initiations. The Eckankar fear never came true for me. I have had a blessed life with a lot more spiritual growth since I left it. Fear motivates people to act irrationally, and we need to be aware of others who try to manipulate us with fears and place us in their ego prisons.

Has anyone ever tried to manipulate you with fear to do or not to do something?

> ### Don't Let Military Boots of Fear and Control March through Your Mind

Fear Loss of Things

The ego loves things and forms strong attachments to them. When people lose things, it can get them so upset that they act irrationally. I was burglarized about 30 years ago in Kentucky, and I was upset about losing things I was attached to. I felt angry and uneasy about burglars violating my personal space and about the state police not doing anything about it even though we knew who did it. Fortunately, I did not become irrational and follow through with the angry thought of burning down their house.

More recently, when our home was burglarized in Minnesota, my reaction was different. I was not attached to the stuff that was stolen since they were just things. I have to admit that I did have attachment to one thing. A necklace my father gave my wife, which was hand-cut from an old coin. My father is deceased now and I felt a sentimental attachment to it since he created it, but even this attachment passed away quickly.

These experiences told me that I was making some progress over ego's attachments. After the Minnesota burglar was caught, I learned that he burglarized houses in Oregon and would burn them down. I wondered how my previous thoughts in Kentucky of wanting to burn down the crook's house almost brought me dangerously close to receiving the karmic consequences of my own house being burnt down.

Do you find yourself overly attached to something and emotionally react if its loss is threatened?

Fear of the Future

Fear of my financial future is probably my strongest fear. Most of my complaining was motivated by this fear. Not knowing what was going to happen in my financial future still pushes my reactions buttons, but not like it used to.

***

I asked why I had such a fear of my financial future while using one of Brian L. Weiss's CDs to do a past life regression. In the experience, I was looking at my feet and they were the feet of a black man. I was thin and wore a Caribbean shirt and shorts. It seemed I was on the borderline of being poor and lived alone in a thatched house. I had a treasure box that had all of my earthly valuables in it and I seemed to be taking an inventory of them and admiring my possessions.

The next scene, I was in my house and robbers were try-ing to get me to tell where I hid my treasure box. I refused to tell them. The next thing I knew they cut off my right leg at the knee with a machete, so I gave them what they wanted. The third sce-ne was as a one-legged, homeless old man begging in the streets. I assumed, I couldn't do whatever work I had done before and had to become a beggar with only one good leg.

Wow! If that wouldn't put the fear of the future in me, I don't know what would. It was an experience that instilled the fear of a negative future in my consciousness, and I'm still feeling the effects of it in this lifetime. Most fears are rooted in past lives.

***

Experiencing this past life, helped me understand my fear at a deeper level, but it did not automatically dispel my fear of the future. When the financial fear arises now, I use this past life experience to help stop the fear from spreading like a wild fire. I tell it, "what happened in a past life doesn't mean it has to hap-pen now. My future is going to be fine." Instead of letting the ego react, I trust the Divine to do what is best for all. This stops the energy of the fear from reaching my crown chakra at the top of the head. It serves as a roadblock to the fear and its irrational behaviors that shut off the flow of divine love and wisdom com-ing into me.

The ego loves to live in the past or future. Since I liked to live in the future, it tends to increase the fear of uncertainty. I tend to view my financial future as negative, but I also view the future as an opportunity for change that can bring good into my life. This makes the present a means to an end. Eventually, I learned, especially after reading Eckhart Tolle's book *The Power of Now,* that my focus should be on the present moment rather than using it as a means for realizing a successful future. *The ego self is past and future-based.* Being spiritual is now-based.

The future and past is where worrying originates. When I focused on the future, it almost always led to worrying in the present. Now that I know the Divine will take care of the future if I take care of the present moment, I don't worry.

Living in the Present Is a No Worry Zone

Do you fear the uncertainty of your future?

Fear of God

I took my mother who was in her 90s to a grocery store and wanted to park as close to the door as possible to make it easier for her. I was waiting for a car to pull out and saw a car next to where we were waiting that had the sign, "FEAR GOD," on its back window. I thought to myself, what about the scripture that says the first commandment is to love God. The next thing I knew the woman who was putting groceries into that car came over and shoved a pamphlet through the window into Mom's hand. I thought that was kind of pushy and rude.

I can remember when I believed in the wrath of God and feared Him. When difficulties came into my life, I thought it was God doing it. Most of the time, I could not connect it to any sin I had committed and wondered why God was punishing me. God's wrath was like the random force of luck that I never knew when or why I would receive it. Random punishment was an effective way of putting the fear of God in me.

I'm glad I eventually realized my relationship with God should not be based on fear. It should be love. I feel sorry for those who live their life imprisoned in this religious dogma of the fear of God. There are enough ego fears and we do not need religions to pile more on top of what already exists. God is pure love and wants a relationship with us based on pure love.

I saw on a church marquee a week before Easter that read, "We use duct tape to fix things. God uses nails." I could feel the pain of nails piercing my hands and feet and it made me sick to my stomach. I thought, that was an awful cruel thing to say, and besides the Divine uses love to fix things. If I didn't know better, that imagery of God pounding nails into my hands and feet would have made me fear God earlier in life when I was a Christian.

If fear is the bases of your relationship with the Divine, I would suggest start looking for another religion or just be the most loving person you can be. *Where there is love, fear cannot exist.*

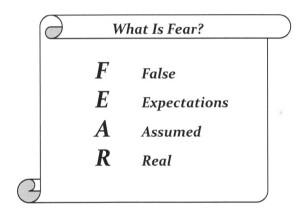

What Is Fear?	
F	*False*
E	*Expectations*
A	*Assumed*
R	*Real*

This is not a comprehensive list of fears, but some that you may recognize happening in your own life. Recognizing them is important for controlling the ego consciousness.

Ego Reacts Unconsciously to Protect Itself

The problem with the ego consciousness is that those who are under its influence do not know it. They are literally in the dark. I was for a long time unaware of the power the ego had over my life and learned about a fuller scope of its influence while writing this book. The ego operates in an unconscious re-active mode since its beliefs, values, attitudes, fears, and experiences are stored in the subconscious mind, the part of the mind that automatically and unconsciously reacts to life's cir-cumstances. *Ego self is unconscious and reactive-based.*

When this happens, the ego self is in full control. We are operating out of what cognitive neuroscientists refer to as the subconscious mind. This is the storehouse were unconscious thoughts, beliefs, emotions, instincts, fears, and habits reside that determine most of our behavior.

According to Bruce H. Lipton and Steve Bhaerman in the book *Spontaneous Evolution,* the subconscious mind controls ap-proximately "95 percent of our decisions, actions, emotions, and behaviors." That's most of what we do. Since the subconscious mind operates by unconscious habits, compulsions, reactions, and drives, we are very much like programmed robots reacting to life's external circumstances. Consequently, we end up being slaves to the automatic responses of the ego's habits stored in the subconscious mind, which blocks our connection with the Di-vine.

In the book, *The Biology of Belief,* Bruce H. Lipton, a cell biologist, characterizes the subconscious mind as a powerful pro-cessor of information. It can process 20 million stimuli from the external environment per second while the conscious mind can only process 40 bits of stimuli per second. Is it any wonder we are more like a robot that automatically responds to external commands than being a highly conscious, self-directed person? The powerful subconscious mind can easily take over your life with the ego habits stored there. This unconscious behavior works against being a conscious spiritual person. Fortunately, there is one way to overcome or eliminate the ego's unconscious power by storing spiritual habits in the subconscious mind.

Filling a Subconscious Mind with Spiritual Habits Leaves No Room for Ego's Habits

The purpose of the ego self is to assure the continual survival of its illusionary identity and ego realities. To accomplish this, it must do whatever is necessary to protect itself. My complaining assumed others (my wife) were at fault, and I was the victim. Consequently, my ego reacted by complaining to assert power over my wife and to protect my ego and maintain its illusion that she caused our financial insecurity.

Ego Is Insecure and Struggles to Protect Itself

My complaining judged my wife as the source of our financial problems while protecting my ego's superior status. Counter attacks on my righteous ego seemed unfair and was like being machine-gunned to death with bullets of guilt that made me feel like a victim. The ego hates and fears whatever threatens its illusions. To protect itself the ego reacts and tries to attack others through anger, complaining, gossip, guilt, vanity, and other ego responses.

There will be a natural tendency for you as a reader to react to some of the things I am saying about the ego especially when it applies to you. If you find yourself reacting, take note of it since it might be one of those unconscious ego habits you will need to deal with at some point in your life.

How do you defend your ego self?

LOG EYE

I'd rather see splinters in other's eyes,
   Rather than the petrified log in my eye.

My ego protects the log,
   Like a ferocious watchdog.

While only the Light of love can replace my log.
   Like the sun's light dissipates fog.

Since the ego is stored within the subconscious and unconsciously reacts with negative responses such as greed, fear, conflict, unhappiness, and dogma it is the reasons for the ego being the enemy from within. We are living in the Ego Age where we have arrived at an evolutionary place in history where the ego has become so dangerous and dysfunctional that it is the enemy that may lead to our extension. However, you have a choice that can change this dangerous trend.

One of the major choices in life is to determine what you want as your true identity. Will it be the ego self or Divine Self? Too many choose the ego and this is why today's world is so unhappy, violent, polarized, and filled with negativity. There is a great need to topple the ego self from its throne of dominance and replace it with the Divine Self. This is the topic of the next chapter.

Figure 3.1

**SUGGESTED QUESTIONS FOR PERSONAL
AND GROUP DISCUSSION**

1. Have you had an experience where love set you free from your ego's habits?
2. Have you ever tried stopping an ego habit that damaged relationships with others?
3. What is your main attachment in life?
4. Do you fear abandonment?
5. Do you fear losing your social status or self-worth?
6. Do you fear losing your body or physical appearance?
7. Do you fear loss of power?
8. Do you fear the loss of some of your most prized material possessions?
9. Do you fear the uncertainty of the future?
10. What other types of fears do you have?
11. How do you control your fears?
12. Are you ego-realized?

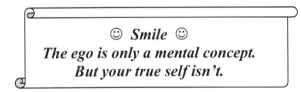

☺ *Smile* ☺
The ego is only a mental concept.
But your true self isn't.

Chapter Four

Being Spiritual Evolves from the Divine Within

I wasn't a rebellious youth, but as a teenager, I felt a hollow emptiness in my life as well as in the lives of my parents, which I mentioned earlier. I was probably uncomfortable with my ego identity as well as with my parent's lack of religion. I sensed something was missing, but I didn't know for sure what it was.

One Easter Sunday, when I was thirteen or fourteen, I decided to attend the local Methodist church. I took my younger brother with me for moral support since I didn't know what to expect.

This church experience led to a different view of who I was. I learned I was born in sin and was a sinner. I felt my body was the devil incarnated. I was taught that sex was a sin even to have a child. In contrast, Eckhart Tolle, a modern day spiritual teacher, believes sex is a spiritual desire for oneness with the Divine. In his book *The Power of Now* he said, "Sexual union is the closest you can get to this state [oneness] on the physical level. This is why it is the most deeply satisfying experience the physical realm can offer." This view is a galaxy apart from what I was taught as a Christian.

I was a sinner and had to believe in Jesus who died for my sins. If I felt guilty enough and repented, my sins were forgiven and I was saved to go to Heaven.

Later in life, I learned that this belief of being a sinner in need of salvation was not something Jesus taught. It was added as a doctrine to try to make sense of Jesus' crucifixion. The church also used it to gain control of its members by making them feel guilt about their sin of killing Jesus. This was an example of how the ego consciousness of church leaders used fear and guilt to control its members.

Religious Beliefs Can Negatively Affect Your Self Image

Soul was another aspect of my identity that Christianity taught, but it was confusing to me as a teenager. The church said I had a soul, something like an invisible spirit that hangs around waiting for me to die. I also learned I would be this soul for the rest of eternity. While living on Earth, I was the ego self with a spiritual appendage hanging around to slip into after death. I therefore believed I was a body that had a soul rather than being a Soul that has a body, and soul was of no importance as a source of identity while living. At least, I was introduced to the belief that there was another part of me that would be spiritual someday.

The church's belief about the end of time where my physical body would rise from the grave in its physical form to be with Jesus was an additional confusion. I wondered. Would I be my body or soul at the end of time? Since the church was attached to the physical form of the body and its ego identity, I thought I might have a physical body in the afterlife after all.

***

Years later, when I worked as a Job Corps teacher in North Carolina, I had a supervising principal who belonged to the Lion's Club. He asked others and me to donate our eyes when we died. When I signed to donate mine, he told me about a man who refused to sign.

The man said to him, "I need my eyes when I rise from the grave at the end of time to be with Christ."

That's how I would have probably believed earlier in my life and might have refused to donate my eyes too. Even though I was confused about whether I would ultimately be spirit or human flesh in the spiritual worlds, I still identified myself with my earthly body, ego mind, and emotions. My Christian beliefs about being soul after death didn't do much to change my identity but it did confuse me. As a Methodist and Quaker, I viewed myself primarily as the ego self.

***

I wish I had the Internet when I was younger since I could have read about Henry's innovative way of how to get into Heaven. He found a loophole to get in with his ego fully intact. Henry's mother was exasperated with his mischievous behavior and asked him, "How do you expect to get into heaven, Henry?"

Henry thought for a while and said, "Well, I'll run in and out, and in and out, and keep slamming the door until St. Peter says, 'For Heaven's sake, Henry, come in or stay out!'"

***

Another church belief I had about the human body was that it had the same image as God. Consequently, I thought God was an old white man with a beard. Not only would soul look like my body, but God looked human too. I didn't realize it at the time that my church was attached to the outer form of the body that would not only exist in the physical world but in the afterlife as well.

This was probably why Archie Bunker and George Jefferson of the *All in the Family* TV program, one of my favorite old time shows, differed about how God looked. In one of the episodes Archie Bunker told George, "Every one of the pictures I've seen, God is white."

George Jefferson quickly retorted, "Maybe you're looking at the pictures' negatives."

Soul and Psychology

The next time I questioned my identity was as a student at West Virginia Wesleyan College. In my psychology class, the professor gave a lecture about personal identity. He talked about the body, mind, emotions, personality, and some social aspects that identified the self. For some reason, I reacted to what he was saying and asked him after class, "Where does soul fit into the picture?"

Since this was a class in a Methodist college, I thought soul should have something to do with my identity. But his response was, "In psychology, we do not deal with soul. It's outside the parameters of scientific investigation."

He didn't dare acknowledge that we became soul after death as the church taught. Even in a religious college, science can ignore soul by defining it out of its realm of investigation. I didn't realize then that I was carrying around some kind of inner awareness that who I was had something to do with being Soul. It wasn't until much later in life that the issue of my true identity surfaced.

Most psychological and social sciences are dogmatic about the existence of the ego identity and ignore Soul, our true identity. Most university scientist, regardless of their ego beliefs about having open minds, operate like a faith-based church and refuse to consider the possibility of a Divine Self. Fortunately, there are some transpersonal psychologists and sociologists and a few others in academic institutions that consider humans as spiritual beings. There is at least a small light of understanding shining in our academic institutions.

Ego Transformation

In the early 1970s, I learned in Eckankar™, which was based on Shabda Yoga that I didn't *have* a soul, but I *am* Soul right now. I didn't have to wait until after death to become Soul. I was already Soul, a divine being.

I also learned that Soul was an eternal spark of God. Therefore, I was a being with divine qualities, and Soul was my primary and everlasting identity. Soul existed from one incarnation to another but took on different body shells that allowed me to operate in the world of matter. This was possibly, what I knew intuitively earlier in my life, which stirred my search for religion and caused me to question my psychology professor. Initially, I only knew myself as a mental concept of being Soul. It took years of spiritual experiences to learn more about myself as Soul. I'm still trying to fully realize and practice that I AM SOUL.

Once I realized I was Soul, my beliefs changed. I now believed that Soul, and not the body, was what the Bible meant when it said we were "made in the image of God." Soul is spirit or pure energy and this is the image of God rather than being a physical looking body.

I was also taught earlier in Christianity that "the body was the temple of the living God," but I did not understand what the "living God" meant. I now know that Soul is the "living God" that lives within the body's temple. This body/temple housed the "living God." When I viewed the body as a temple, it was no longer a sinful thing. The Bible and church doctrine had contradictory beliefs about who I was and I prefer to believe I'm in the image of the "living God."

Since I had to take care of my physical house to have a healthy body, I also learned I had to take care of my body as the home of Soul. Soul needs a clean house or temple with no ego distractions in order to be a focused and joyful resident living in the presence of the Divine.

The body's value was in giving Soul a temporary, earthly temple where it could help function as the Divine's legs and arms in a material world. I have also come to believe that the body's cells also have their share of divine awareness and serve as one of our spiritual partners in the co-creative process.

An unhealthy body makes Soul's work more difficult. That is why the body sends warning signals of pain when we are not taking care of it. Pain is a throbbing warning sign telling us to learn, change, or heal something to allow pure energy to balance the body back to health.

Over time, I gradually deflated my negative ego identity and came to know myself as a Divine Self. I am a divine energy spark from the Divine Source. I will never be God, but may become divine-like. It took me a while, but I now know – I am Soul.

I'm Soul

Experiencing the Golden Energy Soul

Sometime during the latter part of the 1970s, I attended a seminar where there were several thousand in attendance. After 15 or 20 minutes into the session, I looked out over the crowd from the back of the auditorium. I felt uplifted. The collective consciousness of the group helped produce heightened vibrations within me. My focus on physical objects turned blurry, and I saw dark outlines of images of people sitting or walking. A golden hue filled the auditorium. I had experienced the golden hue before at other group meetings and when I was alone, but this time something different happened.

I began to see bright, sparkling golden globes of light that were a little smaller than the size of a volleyball situated close to the back of the heads of a few people. This brilliant golden light emanating from them reminded me of a dynamo of creative liquid energy, and I could feel its peace and love. It emanated the most brilliant golden color I had ever seen.

The other people were like dark shadows without any sign of these golden spheres. I wondered, why did a few have a golden light while others didn't? I noticed some of these dark shadow people were walking toward the front of the auditorium to find seats even though the session had started. Maybe they were thinking like the ego does about being me-deep into themselves and didn't mind disturbing others to get a seat up front.

When I returned to every-day consciousness, I asked myself, what did I just see? I thought about possible explanations of what those brilliant spheres of golden light and energy might be.

I had seen the soft golden hue encompassing the auditorium at previous times but not the bright, golden spheres behind people's heads. I believed the golden hue was the inner Light of the Soul dimension. However, these brilliant spheres of golden light that I saw didn't seem to be an inner plane or dimension.

Was I seeing a golden halo like the ones in pictures surrounding the heads of Jesus and other saints? If so, they didn't encircle the head like halos I had seen in paintings. They were more like an imperfectly shaped sphere situated behind and toward the top of the head.

After the session, I told my wife about this experience, but she didn't know what those spheres were either. Since they were golden, I suspected that they might have something to do with the soul body, but it was only a guess. The bodies with the dark shadows might have been the ones whose ego imprisoned their golden Divine Self inside the body. Since I wasn't sure what

I saw, I didn't tell others about my experience for fear they might think I went a little off the deep side. Since my wife already knew it, telling her didn't matter.

***

When I attended West Virginia Wesleyan College as a student, there was mandatory chapel attendance every week. During my last two years there, I refused to attend most of them even though I would lose some of my course credits. The ego resentment against forced chapel attendance carried over to Westminster College where I was a faculty member. Even though attendance wasn't required at chapel, I did not attend a chapel service during the six years I taught there until the last week just before leaving

I sat behind the Chaplin of the college and since the pews were close, his head was probably a foot or so from my face. At one point during the service, the chapel was filled with a golden hue, and when I looked at the head of the Chaplin seated in front of me, he had the brightest golden sphere I had ever seen. This brightness might have occurred since I sat so close to him or maybe it was an exceptionally bright Soul body. I didn't expect a Christian clergy who was mainly involved in outward rituals and dogmatic beliefs to have such a shining golden Soul. This experience jolted me into learning a lesson about judging the spirituality of a group of people. Spiritual growth is a personal experience and not limited or excluded from any religious or nonreligious Souls.

***

Soul Body Can Be Seen as Golden Light

Spiritual experiences or observations were usually not completely understood at the time of my experience and I had to

62

go through a period where I had to interpret them. After having experiences of the golden soul for several years or more at other group meetings and at home, I reached a more satisfying interpretation. I concluded that I was seeing the Divine Self or what some refer to as the Soul body. It was the manifestation of Soul as golden light or energy, but it was only the form image and not the full aspect of what Soul is.

I had heard that Plato saw Soul as a golden entity residing near the head of a person or following them from a distance. He also said Soul could be entrapped inside the body. Maybe those with an entrapped Soul were the people I saw as dark shadows.

***

How many enlightened Souls does it take to screw in a light bulb? None or possibly one. Since they can use their own "Inner Light," they do not need external lights. Or since enlightened people do what is good-for-All, they are happy to install a light bulb to help others see.

***

I don't want to give the impression that the golden Soul body is all that Soul is. Soul is a divine being and is therefore omnipresent. It is not confined to our heads, but consciousness can be anywhere it focuses its attention. It is all-present in the physical and spiritual worlds. The focusing of conscious attention determines where and what Soul experiences.

I'm not just my physical body, achievements, accumulation of material things, social and career status, mental capabilities, and other such ego based things. More importantly, I'm a divine being and so is everyone else. If you want to love the Divine, love yourself as the Divine Self. Since we are of the likeness of the Divine, we are divine-like. If you are searching for the Divine, it will end with the spiritual image of your own Soul. I would also like to add that our divine likeness or essence appears as brilliant, golden atoms of the divine's manifested energy.

63

> ### We Are Golden Sparkling Energy Atoms of the Divine

Have you ever had an experience where you felt you were more than your physical or ego body?

A major paradigm shift in consciousness from the ego self to the Divine Self is needed. This will create changes in individual lives, which will be followed by changes in the collective consciousness of the world. This outcome, however, depends on whether people like you choose to be spiritual.

Have you decided to be spiritual?

> ### Soul, the Golden Sparkling Atom of the Divine
>
> *I once thought I was a sinful, worldly ego self,*
>   *Imprisoned in a physical body of matter.*
>
> *When I saw the vibrant, golden sparkling self,*
>   *I knew I was more than the ego and mind's clatter.*
>
> *I'm Divine golden energy atoms and one with the whole,*
>   *And thankful I'm a free golden sparkling Soul.*

Most humans are the only creatures refusing to recognize who they are. What matters is not success in the social world, but realizing your true self as Soul. Do you believe your true self is the ego self? If so, do as little Mary did and repeat the affirmation – "I'm sole." Or better yet, say, "I'm Soul." Just know that the answer to the question - "Who am I?" - is Soul, the golden spark of Divine Energy.

> *We're Created with the Divine's Happy Face,*
> *But Prefer the Ego's Mean False Face*

The next two chapters will discuss the second shift. It is a shift from the ego consciousness of a separate material being from others to being divine energy and unified with others and the Divine. In these two chapters, you will discover that you are an energy being with powerful energy tools.

Figure 4.2

SUGGESTED QUESTIONS FOR PERSONAL AND GROUP DISCUSSION

1. What is your answer to the question "Who am I?"
2. Did your perception of who your true self was change during your lifetime? If so, how?
3. Do you now view your true self as Soul or the Divine Self?
4. Have you ever experienced the golden energy body of Soul?
5. What is the basic motivation in your life?
6. How do you create the things you want in your life?
7. Have you experienced Soul being the conscious observer of your ego habits?
8. Have you ever used Soul's power of just being something you wanted to be?
9. Have you ever experienced being one with the Divine?

☺ *Smile* ☺
You're a divine golden energy being.
Have you discarded your ego's rags and false face?

SHIFT II

Ego Polarization to Spiritual Unity

The ego self views its identity as a physical and mental entity that is separate from other humans, animals, plant life, earth's environment, and the Divine. Separation creates polarization and the desire to dominate, which is evident with today's political parties and dissension throughout the world. Humans at their quantum level are energy beings and made of the same energy that is in all life and earthly materials. When viewed from the perspective of being quantum energy fields, the realization of spiritual oneness is possible, and this becomes the basis for unity and living in peace with all life and environments. We are energy beings or fields connected to ever-broadening energy fields, which units us at the quantum level rather than how the ego views itself as separate at the physical level. A shift from ego polarization to spiritual unity and harmony is needed to be spiritual.

Chapter Five

You Are an Energy Being Connected with Others

Albert Einstein revolutionized the understanding of energy with his formula $E=mc^2$. It basically, tells us that "energy" (E) equals "mass" (m) times the speed of light squared (c^2). In essence, the solid appearance of all material forms such as tables, houses, bodies, etc. are energy atoms at their quantum level held together by universal forces. In the last four chapters, we discussed the body, ego, and the Divine Self, which are nothing more than energy fields. You, therefore, are in essence an energy being.

When my family helped edit this chapter, my wife read this section just before she had cataract surgery. Not being a scientist, she read the formula $E=mc^2$ as "E = me too." We all laughed, but it was a spiritual truth channeled through her to remind us that we were all energy too.

The formula also informs us that energy can be transformed into mass or material things and material things can be transformed back into energy. Just like the destruction at Hiroshima turned an ounce of material plutonium into an atomic energy bomb.

Universe Is Nothing More than Energy Include Me Too

***

I suppose Einstein did not know how universal his formula was since it can be applied to the ego as well as spiritual energy. For example, *Ego energy (E)* = Mankind (*m*) X Conflict² (*c²*). The formula also applies to *Spiritual energy (E)* = Mankind (*m*) X Cooperation² (*c²*). Although these appear to be true statements, Einstein is probably rolling over in his grave wondering how these formulas would ever be quantified.

Human Beings Are Energy Beings

Everything in the universe derives from unmanifested energy, which is derived from the Divine Source. The Divine Energy and Divine Self are also realms where the unmanifested or formless energy exists. At these levels of spirituality, we are in a state of oneness and unity with all. We are derived from unity, but when we enter the world of duality where the ego exists, we shift into a state of separateness and polarization. A spiritual being strives to return to its original state of oneness and unity.

As the unmanifested energy emerges from its sources, it transforms into different manifested forms of matter in the worlds of duality. This includes the dimensions of the subtle energy fields, physical body, mental and emotional fields, and all other physical matter. Even matter is derived from the unmanifested energy of the Divine Source, which means that it is in a state of unity and oneness with all other matter. We are therefore derived from one common energy source and have oneness with all types of matter as well as spirit.

When this oneness with all is realized, we know we are in a state of unity with all. It is the mental ego energy that believes

70

itself to be separate from others as well as its physical and spiritual environments.

Being an energy being with oneness with all is one of the little known aspects about who we are. The ego focuses on the physical body and the spiritual energy and Divine Self goes unnoticed. The biological, social, and psychological sciences primarily focus attention on the body and its unconscious mental, emotional, and social aspects without realizing it as a source of energy with transformative spiritual powers. It is time to shift our consciousness to the realization of the unity experienced by the Divine Self and away from the egos desires for separateness, conflict, and polarization.

Interconnected Energy Fields

Fortunately, quantum physics, evolutionary biology, and other research began opening up the hidden identity of who we are as energy beings. During the last century, quantum physics questioned the basic premises of Newton's classical physics concerning its focus on physical matter being separate from other forms of matter.

At the subatomic level, electrons circle neutrons and protons at high speeds and at great distances from each other. When nuclear and electromagnetic forces bind these energy entities together, they form atoms. Atoms are at the root of what makes a body, which are dynamos of energy or quantum energy fields. These energy atoms are 90 to 99.9 percent empty space but appear as solid matter when they become entangled with each other. In reality, they are only energy with a lot of empty space.

I'm not sure if it's true since I have not experienced it nor has science verified it, but the *Kryon* books believe this empty space is the storage place for the love force in the universe. If this is true, every atom is a storehouse of love energy, which makes the power of love plentiful and vastly available.

Be Spiritual

The body has trillions of cells, but I have not seen any estimate of the number of atoms in a human body. The number would be mind-boggling. To build the human body, atoms are entangled and cooperate and combine to form cells, organs, and body systems (e.g., nervous, vascular, and digestive), which are interrelated energy fields increasing in size. It was interesting when I learned that x-rays and MRIs do not take pictures of bones or organs, but they are taking pictures of the energy fields of these body parts.

In the book, *Earth Dance* by Elisabet Sahtouris, an evolutionary biologist, she explains how we are living in an ever increasing interconnected layer of fields from the smallest form of life to the Earth and universe itself. Life is a dance of these connected partners of fields, which affect each other and are usually living in harmony instead of dominating and exploiting each other. If we continue the ego way of domination, we will receive the consequences of our unwise actions of harming the balanced interconnections in nature and all life. Realizing how we are united is the way of spirituality.

Fields in the body and surrounding the body as subtle energy bodies are interrelated with other fields. We are interconnected in an ever-widening expansion of energy fields. We are not separate entities, but are connected with other energy fields, which makes it possible for us to adversely or beneficially affect each other. Energy systems unite in greater fields of interconnection from the micro, to the physical body, to the universe, and ultimately connected to the Divine Source itself. The ego as a separate entity is simply not true. We and the rest of the world are broadening circles of interconnected energy fields or systems.

The amazing thing is how all of these energy fields are coordinated to create and maintain a balanced state of life working in harmony without any of our conscious efforts to make it happen. This is the model of cooperation and peace humans should model in their social relationships and learn to be in balance and harmony with all other energy fields.

***

One day, when I watched the Dr. Oz Show on TV, he talked about how to lose belly fat. I was very interested in this since I have a stomach that blows up like a balloon with lightning speed, but it is very difficult and slow to flatten it.

I had success one time in reducing my belly fat, but recently I can't find an easy way to do it. According to Bruce H. Lipton, a microbiologist, in *The Biology of Belief* book, thoughts can affect DNA. When I head this, I decided to talk to the fat DNA cells in my belly and tell them they were no longer needed. I told them, "I no longer live in the age of hunting and gathering when belly fat was needed for periods of food shortages, and I want you to dissolve yourself and pass out of my body." Unfortunately, I have found that my belly fat cells were either really dumb, couldn't understand English, or were rebellious teenager cells refusing to listen. They didn't want to go away.

I talk aloud to them when I'm alone and when no one is around. As I'm writing this, I'm hoping there are no psychiatrists reading this book since I'm not sure if talking to fat cells is a sign of having a more serious mental problem than talking to God. I just want to let them know that I have never heard my fat cells talk back to me, so please do not send a paddy wagon to get me.

And for the rest of the Dr. Oz's belly fat story. One of the devices he demonstrated was a laser that burst fat cells, which eventually passed them out of the body. The woman who demonstrated the machine said it took a few sessions with the laser to dissolve some of the fat cells and then the fat cells started communicating with each other to instruct the other fat cells to dissolve on their own. I thought this was a neat example of how cells were interrelated, able to communicate, and cooperated with each other. I wish my fat belly cells would start listening and pass the exodus information to my other cells since I can't afford the some $3,000 for the laser work.

***

Chapter 1 included an illustration of the subtle body energy fields that surround the physical body. They mediate energy between Soul and the body. This adds another layer of energy fields that vibrate higher than physical energy fields and because of this; the human eye cannot see them. They include the etheric or intuitive, emotional, memory, and mind energy fields that are referred to by some as the human aura. In addition, there is the Divine Self energy field, which should be in charge of all the other subtle and human energy fields.

People with high-level energy vibrations can see these energy fields as light and hear them as sound. Subtle body fields provide the life force energy, which does much of the coordination of the zillions of things needed to maintain life.

Additionally, there are collective energy fields of social groups. The Earth itself has an energy field, which is known as the earth's magnetic field. All of these fields interact with each other and can affect each other according to Elisabet Sahtouris.

You as an energy being extend your energy influence much farther than the boundary of your outer skin. This is why it is important for you to be the best spiritual person of love and peace you can be. Since your energy fields also affect the energy fields of the family, co-workers, friends, community, nation, and even the world, what you think, feel, imagine, and do is important. If you change to be spiritual, the world is also affected.

> ### *Energy Is Borrowed and Should Be Given Back with Love Interest Added*

The energy fields that exist inside and outside of you: provide the life force that creates and maintains life, provides a doorway to direct divine experiences, holds the key to co-create with divine thoughts, is the home of your Divine Self, connects us to each other, and can change the world. You are of utmost importance for world peace, joy, and freedom when you are spiritual with all of this connectivity.

Experiencing Energy Fields

For most of my life, I was ignorant of energy fields. I had some experiences later that helped me understand some things such as the golden energy field of the Divine Self. It wasn't until I wrote this book that I began to understand its fuller importance for my spiritual life and the Love Age.

I believe the first time I heard about auras was when Audrey introduced me to Edgar Cayce's books. He could see the colored lights produced by energy fields emanating around the bodies of people. He used these auras to pinpoint health problems and was able to suggest remedies for restoring health. I can remember wishing I could experience seeing auras.

Eventually, I was able to see them. I never had much control over this type of experience except when I squinted my eyes or received help from a group's higher vibration level. The experience was also usually spontaneous. I can't remember the first time I saw an aura, but there were a few experiences that stood out.

***

In the mid-1990s, I worked for the State of California. One day my boss was sitting in a chair conducting a departmental meeting. I sat on the other side of the table listening to her. My eyes started to go out of focus and a green colored light surrounded the top part of her body, since that was the only part I could see above the level of the table. It lasted about a minute and disappeared as my eyes returned to a clear focus of the room. I saw this aura several other times at meetings.

I wondered why I only saw a green aura as the predominate color surrounding her. I recalled from Edgar Cayce's books that green related to people who pursued medical professions, but she wasn't in that field. In Shabda Yoga, the color green related to the earth plane consciousness, and she was very much oriented toward ego worldly success.

Another experience happened about a decade or so ago when I was at a worship service in Sacramento. A person that I respected for her spirituality and loving nature was speaking about a personal experience. As she talked, I saw a golden aura surrounding her whole body. It was not like the sphere of golden light at the back of the head that I mentioned previously. The predominate color was golden on the outer ring, but there were other colors on the inner rings that were faint, which made it difficult to discern. Gold light for me represented Soul, the Divine Self. I could understand why I saw a golden aura around this loving Soul.

Auras Are Energy Fields

Have you ever seen an aura?

***

One of the strangest auras I ever saw was the aura of a tall pine tree. I moved to a new home in the Sierra Mountains surrounded by tall cedar and white pine trees. My son and I packed and unpacked the truck in the same day. If the neighbors had seen me slowly climb the two flights of stairs at the end of the move, they might have wondered if I was a 120-year-old man ready to kill over. I was at the point of total exhaustion.

I wondered, was this move worth the effort? On Monday, I had to start an hour commute to work. Did Audrey and I make a mistake moving here?

Being among tall pine trees had always given me a sense of inner peace and was one of the main reasons for moving there.

Even though I was exhausted, I decided to view the tall trees from the back patio before dusk turned to nighttime. When I leaned my aching body on the patio banister, my eyes began to blur. I wondered if I was going to faint. One pine tree stood out from the others, and I could see a light bluish and green color light surrounding the outline of it. The light looked similar to the bluish/green flames of a gas-burning fireplace.

I blinked my eyes thinking something must be in them, but the flaming colors were still there. I then received a telepathic thought - "All will be fine." What did this mean, I wondered? My eyes came back in focus and I moved over to one of the patio chairs to rest my weary bones.

I had heard about long distant runners getting so exhausted that they entered altered states of consciousness. Did this happen to me when I saw the tree's aura? I had seen auras around people before, but I never saw an aura around plant life. Was it the tree's aura? Then I turned my attention to the message that "All will be fine." Did that mean the move was the right thing to do even though the commute to work would be a longer one? I sure hoped so.

Later, I came to the conclusion that the tree channeled a divine message to comfort me. It also made me aware that the Divine could use anything to give messages of guidance, help, and comfort.

After about a year had passed, I watched a television movie about Moses that had a scene where he saw a burning bush and received a message from it. It brought back the memory of a childhood Sunday school class where I learned about Moses and saw a picture in a study guide of a burning bush as thought it was engulfed in flames. At that time, I thought it was impossible for a bush to burn, continue to live, and talk to Moses. I didn't believe this story at all.

When I remembered my own aura experience of the pine tree looking like it was outlined in a bluish/green flame, I won-

dered. Did Moses see a flame-like aura around the bush as I did?
That seemed to be a better explanation than a bush on fire.

***

We are not the only thing in the world that has an aura or
energy field surrounding it. Since everything is energy, everything has auras and can be used to interrelate with other fields
and the Divine can use them to communicate with us.

Followers of Hinduism, Buddhism, Christian mystics,
Jewish Kabbalah, Mayan, Cherokee, Incan, and other spiritual
groups have reported seeing auras or light surrounding the body.
These energy fields were known for thousands of years or even
longer by shamanistic practitioners. It was an integral part of
their lives and healing practices. It is only recently that scientists
have begun to research energy bodies, and Western health practices are also starting to use Eastern energy healing.

My wife is a registered nurse and works at a university
medical hospital that offered a course for nurses in *Reiki* energy
healing. She took the course and found a new outlet for her
compassion for helping others. Some of the nurses in the pediat-
ric ward used it to help children. I'm not suggesting that the
medical center has completely integrated *Reiki* healing into the
hospital's medical practices. They are taking steps toward recognizing the importance of energy as a source of healing beyond its
use in taking x-rays and MRIs. In time, I expect it will be even
more fully integrated in the health systems as it is already used at
other hospitals and clinics. Energy enlivens the body and it also
heals it.

Energy Field Research

Researchers are more aware of physical energy inside the
body than in the energy fields surrounding it. Their ability to
measure physical energy makes this possible. Every cell in the
body is made of atoms and is like a re-chargeable battery that

creates and stores electricity and magnetic energy. All the atoms in a cell operate like a charger pulling energy from the universal source of energy. The cells then store its electric and magnetic field energy for its operations and maintenance. Energy fields exist not only around cells but also around the organs and even the whole body.

Auras and Science

When I first saw auras around people, I wasn't aware I was viewing energy fields or subtle energy bodies. I just thought of it as the Light of God shining around us. Researchers have begun to put together evidence of energy outside the body.

Energy fields surrounding the body are difficult to measure, but researchers have viewed some of their effects and detected the transformation of subtle energy into physical energy into our bodies. Physicists refer to this field of energy surrounding and in our bodies as the Zero Point Field (ZPF). It not only exists in and outside our bodies but in the whole universe.

> *Energy Is Abundant and Omnipresent.*

Cyndi Dale in her book *The Subtle Body* reports that science has used the Superconducting Quantum Interference Device (SQUID) to detect electromagnetic energy beyond the body. In other research, Fritz-Albert Popp and other researchers found that there was a level operating behind DNA's chemical processes. At this level, DNA stored photons, a unit of light, which emits electromagnetic energy and drives the body's processes. They also report that DNA responds to a field of light that surrounds the body.

Fritz-Albert Popp discovered that all life has a shining current of light emanating from it. For example, experiments with cancer patients found their lights were dull and almost going out, but when they observed healthy patients, their biophotons vibrated at a "super powerful frequency" and shined brightly.

I have read that the University of California Davis Center for Biophotonics Science and Technology recently used the power of light energy to image how HIV transmits itself. It was different from what had been theorized, and they now hope this new discovery will direct medical researchers toward new cures for HIV. They are also working on cancer to understand how it operates. It is heartening that energy research like this is expanding our ability to be better healers.

Physical & Spiritual Bodies Are Energy & Emanate Light

Energy fields are sources of light that surround us, which contain information, emotions, thoughts, "life force" energy, memories, spiritual love, among other types of energy. Many refer to this external source of energy as subtle bodies or spiritual energy. Since science has difficulty measuring this external energy directly, its effects have to serve as indirect indicators of it.

Cyndi Dale also reports that Dr. William Tiller, a research physicist at Stanford University, has detected these subtle energy fields surrounding the body. When these subtle energies convert to physical energy, a transducer signal at a magnetic vector detects it. So far, this transformation of energy is a way physical instruments can detect energy fields external to our body. In addition, the magnetic and electrical signals have observable physical effects. Science is only beginning to study the energy aspects of humans, and I hope it expands its research in this area rather than just focusing on the body as physical and chemical processes.

80

Science Ignoring Spiritual Energy Is Like
Light Bulbs Shining without Electricity

Spiritual people know they are energy beings connected to all other energy fields that can help create harmony in the world. The ego believes it's alone in the world and it needs to defend itself, which creates conflict and polarization. One of the highest spiritual experiences is to realize the oneness with all, which arises out of this interconnectedness of all energy fields. The next chapter continues the scientific validation of energy fields as well as how they work to create unity and harmony within and between the biological, environmental, social, and spiritual worlds.

Figure 5.1

**SUGGESTED QUESTIONS FOR PERSONAL
AND GROUP DISCUSSION**

1. Are you aware that you are a being of energy?
2. Have you ever seen an aura around another person?
3. Have you ever tried to go within to feel your energy field that surrounds the body?
4. Have you ever had an energy healing?
5. Have you ever experienced an aura around a plant or animal?

☺ *Smile* ☺
You're a powerful being of energy.
Are you using your energy to expand love in the world?

Chapter Six

Energy Fields and Spiritual Unity

The spiritually enlightened from the past have known that all of us derive from and connect to the unmanifested energy of the Divine Source. We are all made of the same substance. This is at the root of what spiritual masters sought to experience as the oneness with all. This spiritual experience truly provides an inner source of peace and harmony with all others, the environment, and the Divine.

If you are spiritual, this is what you will eventually experience too. The spiritual experiences of the light and sound and spiritual dimensions by enlightened beings have helped validate what scientists are beginning to find. For example, the mathematics of string theory, a more recent development in quantum physics, theorizes that six to eleven dimensions exist beyond our physical world. These dimensions are no more than broad energy fields existing at different levels of spiritual vibrations.

These levels, planes, or dimensions known by spiritual practitioners varied from each other in number, description, and purpose. Since they are subtle energy fields with vague and difficult borders to discern, it is difficult to reach a consensus on their number.

Energy Fields Are also Spiritual Dimensions

The following list of spiritual dimensions is a starting point for our discussion of the energy levels existing beyond the body. I discussed it briefly in the chapters about the Divine Self and ego self and in Figure 1.1. I will list these levels again, and add a few alternative names in brackets.

- Divine Source [God, Divine]
- Divine Energy [Spirit, Holly Ghost, *Reiki*]
- Divine Self [Spiritual Mind, Soul]
- Mental Subtle Body [Intellectual Mind, Analytical Mind]
- Memory Subtle Body [Causal, Instinctive Mind, Subconscious mind]
- Emotional Subtle Body [Astral, Emotions]
- Intuitive Subtle Body [Etheric]
- Physical body [Humans, Nature, Earth]

Spiritual seekers have experienced these energy or spiritual dimensions, and modern science is beginning to discover more about them. Today, more and more people are experiencing and realizing we are more than the world of matter we detect with our senses. These energy fields are elements of our self and need to be realized to understand spirituality. This is especially true since it provides a doorway into the spiritual worlds, provides a source of spiritual wisdom and love, and is the essence that unifies us. Love is the most powerful energy in the universe and these inner spiritual sources of energy are the source of divine love.

Love the Divine Self

Loving the body self,
  Depends on others' approval & its loss is your pain.

Loving the ego self,
  Creates vanity and other's disdain.

Loving the Divine Self,
  Fills your tank with love's high octane.

Transforming Subtle Energy into Physical Energy

Most believe we receive energy only from the food we eat and the oxygen we breathe, but we also receive it from our subtle body's energy fields. How are subtle energy and its information surrounding our body transformed into physical energy and wisdom? Cyndi Dale describes the interface between the subtle energy fields and the body as mediated by channels or meridians throughout the body. These "Rivers of Light" pulsate with vital energy and transport energy into and around the person's body.

The body has organs that convert the subtle energy with high vibrations into lower vibrating energy so it's in a usable form. These organs can be compared to the transformers that reduce electrical power to homes to lower the power of electricity for use in appliances and the computer I'm using to write this book.

Chakras Are the Transformers of Spiritual Energy

Eastern religions refer to these areas where subtle energy enters the body as *chakras*. W. A. Tiller, W. E. Dibble, Jr., and

85

Be Spiritual

J. G. Kohane experimented and found the meridian and *chakra* areas of the body had higher electromagnetic energy when compared to other areas. This suggests that these areas are the places where subtle energy transforms into lower vibrating physical energy. Consequently, *Chakras* are the body's transformers as well as portals into spiritual dimensions.

Figure 6.1

Chakra Centers and Spiritual Energy Functions

CHAK-RAS	*BODY LOCATIONS*	*ENERGY FUNCTIONS*
1	Groin (Base of Spine)	Primal Needs & Physical Existence
2	Abdomen (Ovaries & Testes)	Encourages Creating & Nurturing
3	Solar Plexus (Pancreas)	Need for Information & Power
4	Heart (& Thymus)	For Love & Compassion
5	Throat (Thyroid)	For Higher Wisdom
6	Third-eye on Forehead (Pituitary)	To Bridge the Subtle Realms
7	Crown on top of head (Pineal)	To Dissolve into the Essence of All or Spirit

[Source: Cyndi Dale, *The Subtle Body,* 2009]

The numbers of body *chakras* vary in range from four to twelve, but most use seven. Most Eastern religions also agree that when one progresses in consciousness from the first *chakra* to the seventh at the top of the head, the possibility of experiencing the Divine increases.

In case you are unfamiliar with chakras, the seven most commonly recognized *chakras* were described in Figure 6.1. They are related to the organs and primary spiritual function that are often associated with these incoming and outgoing energy centers.

If you are using these *chakras* for direct spiritual experiences in meditation, I would suggest using the sixth and seventh ones. It is here that you can have the easiest and most direct experiences with the Divine. Not only does energy pour into us at the chakra areas, but it is also the doorway into the subtle energy fields where you can experience inner spiritual dimensions. Eckhart Tolle uses the feeling of the total subtle energy body as a point of focus rather than the individual *chakras* for spiritual experiences. Your focus for meditation practices is your choice since there are multiple doorways to the Divine.

Energy of the Love Age

Individual's energy fields affect the energy level of the collective consciousness. The higher the individual's energy vibrations are and the more people who have these higher levels; the higher the collective vibrations will be. This is what brings a consciousness of peace and love to the planet and will manifest the Love Age. The *Kryon* books channeled by Lee Carroll are filled with information about this increase in vibrations here on Earth and its effect on helping to bring about a higher collective consciousness.

According to *Kryon* the increase in the level of vibrations by humans has created a change in the magnetic grid on Earth where the collective energy of the planet is stored. The grids have been adjusting since the late 1980s, which has been confirmed by science. Some believe the north and south poles will flip-flop, but this will not happen according to *Kryon*. Worldwide, we are experiencing a new level of energy vibrations, but there are some areas where the energy allows for a greater access to spiritual dimensions and wisdom.

One of the areas where this is occurring is on the west coast of North America. I remember hearing Eckhart Tolle saying in a video that when he was in England, he was inwardly directed to move to the west coast. He did not know why he was directed there. When he arrived in Vancouver, Canada, he sat at his kitchen table and wondered why he was there. He thought of returning to England, but he received the guidance to write a book. When he did this, it led to his ground-breaking insights into letting readers know how to increase their spiritual energy vibrations by accessing the now. Later, he realized that it was the energy on the west coast that helped him write *The Power of Now* book.

Lee Carroll is also located on the west coast in the San Diego area. I have come to believe that Carroll and Tolle are the foremost providers of information guiding us into the Love Age. By the way, Tolle calls it the New Earth and Carroll calls it the New Age or The New Jerusalem.

I have been writing my book since 1998, but this was only after I left California for Minnesota. I often wondered why I left the west coast after reading how other authors were positively affected by its vibrations. Possibly, one of the reasons I was directed to live in Minnesota was to be able to attend the Loft Literary Center to learn more about how to write. About twelve years after moving, I read in one of *Kryon's* books a suggestion for people to move to colder climates, and Minnesota sure qualified for that. Maybe the cold Minnesota winters freeze the ego for better access to divine wisdom.

After a time in Minnesota before knowing any of the above information about the west coast vibrations helping authors, my wife and I found a way to live in Minnesota during the summer and in California during the winter. This probably gave me the chance to tap into some of the west coast energy where my writing has been more effective and creative.

Both Tolle and *Kryon* have said that the new energy that is now here will be more stabilized by 2012 to make it easier for people to become enlightened beings at a faster pace. My experiences of trying to be an enlightened being for some 73 years were slow and painful. I use to believe it would be impossible to increase the world's spiritual consciousness since no one would want to take the time or effort to do it. Since the turn of the century, I have however, observed the increase in my own level of spiritual experiences while writing this book. It has increased significantly in comparison to my earlier years, and it is speeding up at an ever-increasing pace.

I also noticed the same pattern of faster spiritual unfoldment among the people I have had the privilege of being in book discussions in Pennsylvania and California. They are spiritually unfolding and this has made me a believer in the increasing pace of spiritual unfoldment with the new energy and consciousness. *Kryon* had channeled that this is a gift we have earned as humans and it will be easier to be dual citizens of the physical and spiritual dimensions as a result.

I've become a believer that this is actually happening and the Love Age has a greater probability of happening more than at any other time in history. Jesus and other spiritual giants tried to do it, but the consciousness of their time did not allow it. Today the consciousness is much higher and growing. I now believe it is my life's purpose to help make this shift in spiritual energy to help bring about the Love Age.

The shift from ego polarization to spiritual unity is one of the needed shifts for you to be spiritual and for the Love Age to be realized. Ego consciousness of "me vs. them" ignites conflicts and polarization, which is so easy to observe in today's political and economic relationships. We need the inner knowingness of oneness with all, which gives the underlying experience for living in unity and cooperation with others.

Realizing the interconnectivity of energy fields emphasizes the commonness we have with other humans and the other environments we interact with. We are interrelated and in unity at the quantum energy level and we should not be in dominating and controlling relationship with other energy fields. Working in cooperation and harmony with them is the way of being spiritual.

I have spent a lot of time on energy, but an understanding of energy is basic to the understanding of spirituality. The next three chapters will discuss the shift from the good-for-me to good-for-All motivations.

Figure 6.2

**SUGGESTED QUESTIONS FOR PERSONAL
AND GROUP DISCUSSION**

1. Have you ever read a scientific study about energy fields that helped validate your spiritual experiences?
2. Have you experienced the power of love energy in your life?
3. Have you ever used *chakras* in your spiritual practices or for healing?
4. Have you noticed that the heightened energy on Earth has made it easier for you or others' spiritual growth?
5. Have you experienced the energy power of your thoughts to co-create things, circumstances, or states of consciousness in your life?
6. Are you aware of how polarized the ego consciousness is in today's world?
7. Have you noticed how humans and the world are becoming more united even though there is increased polarization?

☺ *Smile* ☺
*You're a powerful being of spiritual energy.
Are you using your energy to be spiritual?*

SHIFT III

Good-For-Me to Good-For-All

Most people who operate out of the ego consciousness desire to get what is good-for-me or good-for-others. To be more spiritual, your intentions and actions arise out of what is good-for-All. Doing what's good-for-All is in its essence living a life based on divine love in all your relationships. Shifting from good-for-me to good-for-All motivations is the single most important shift for establishing the Love Age. It is a shift from the fear and conflict of the ego to the love of the spiritual consciousness. Living and making decisions with divine love is the most important shift for being spiritual. It is the motivating essence of the Love Age

Chapter Seven

Amanda Dream – Love's Turning Point

For the first four decades of my life most of what I did or desired was a dilemma between two competing motivations. I wasn't sure whether I should desire things for the good-of-me or for the good-of- others.

In the late 1970s, I started experiencing a lot of mental, physical, and spiritual pain. I think of it as my "dark night of soul," and all I wanted was relief from it. I pleaded that whatever lesson I had to learn would it please quickly show itself. It was not until later in life that I realized these experiences were a turning point for understanding one of the most important aspects of love. It was the most difficult time of my life as well as the most significant turning point in learning to be spiritual.

Nomadic Life

From 1977 to 1979, my family and I accelerated our slow nomadic pace of living. During this period, we moved from New Castle, Pennsylvania, where I taught sociology at Westminster College to Phoenix, Arizona. Then we moved to Marianna, Pennsylvania (my hometown); back west to Boulder, Colorado; and back again to Marianna. After the children finished the school year, we had completed one year of nomadic moving. Our next move was to San Diego, California for the summer months. In the fall we went back east to Hazard, Kentucky where I taught at the University of Kentucky's Community College system for nine months before moving west again to Turlock, California. This made a grand total of nearly seven cross-country moves within a two-year period.

***

Years later when my grandson, Sean, studied nomads in a second or third grade social studies class, his teacher told them. "Nomads are a group of people who move a lot, but they always have one place they call home." Sean raised his hand, and the teacher said, "Sean do you have a question?"

"No. But I think my mother was a nomad when she was young. Her family moved all over the United States, but their home was in Pennsylvania." There's a wise saying that out of the mouths of children, the truth shall be known. Sean accurately viewed his mother, BJ, as a teenage nomad.

***

During the first year of this nomadic life, I was unemployed and tried to decide what new career I should pursue. My ego believed a perfect job was somewhere out there. Also, my wife and I wanted to relocate our family of four children and two dogs, which was like chasing the ego illusion of Shangri-La.

The ego is good at constructing mental and emotional illusions that become unrealistic motivations and create unhappiness when they are not realized. I'll let you in on a little secret about life. There is no perfect job or a Shangri-La in the ego state of consciousness; ego desires at best only create relative satisfaction and most of the time a lot of unhappiness. From a higher spiritual level of awareness, all of the difficult circumstances we find ourselves in are perfect; since they are lessons we created for ourselves to become more enlightened beings.

Our family now laughs about these nomadic escapades. However, while living through them, I experienced emotional, mental, physical, and spiritual pain that made it seem we were traveling through the valley of the shadow of death.

This nomadic experience forced me to look at life at a deeper level and initiated one of life's most significant turning points. It helped answer the basic question of **why** I should be spiritual in the first place. The motivations of my intentions and actions should be for the good-of-all, which is the same as living a life based on love rather than ego's fears or conflicts.

One of the important aspects of life is to understand why you want or desire something since motivations determine the consequences of your actions. When I observed the impact of my frequent moves on the family, especially how they affected the children, I was in a dilemma as to whether I should be living my life for the good-of-me or for the good-of-them. I knew it was right to want what was good-for-others, but how was I to realize my desires?

> *Actions Speak Nothing If You Do Not Know the Motive*

Over time, I've learned that the reason why I do something is more important than the actions I take since intentions are what initiates, directs actions, and attracts the consequences I receive. It is important to be conscious of motivations since awareness determines whether my choices are done with or without love.

Amanda Literature Dream

I had a dream that gave me guidance about how to resolve my dilemma about wanting what's good-for-me versus what's good-for-others. About ten years before starting the intensive nomadic period of my life, I learned that my nightly dreams were important to understand what was going on in my inner and outer lives. At that time, dreams were my primary doorway for receiving divine wisdom. I wrote my dreams down and diligently analyzed them for their hidden messages of wisdom. Surprisingly, a significant spiritual dream made its way through all the negativity I experienced during my "dark night of soul."

***

One evening after living in Boulder, Colorado, for several months, I was in bed and unable to go to sleep. My wife was already asleep. The night light in the hallway shown through the bedroom door and cast shadows off unpacked boxes of books and other household items. Negative thoughts about my six months of unemployment, job rejections, and financial problems occupied my mind. I felt a deep loneliness of living in an uncaring and cruel world where it even seemed the Divine had abandoned me. I was wondering if God had become a mute or maybe even had Alzheimer's and forgot about me.

> *Worries & Stress Are Ego's Garbage. Please, Empty Quickly*

My ego self was on the defensive and reacted to all of the negative garbage I experienced. It dragged me down to one of the lowest victim states of consciousness I had ever experienced. Tears intermittently ran down my cheek and onto the pillow. I kept my head turned from Audrey, my wife, in case she might awaken and see me.

Sometime later, a glimmer of hope crept into my thoughts as I remembered receiving help from past dreams. I wondered if I could possibly receive help from a dream again. Before going to sleep that night, I halfheartedly begged, please show me what career is right for me and help me know what to do to find a job. Please!

The next morning as I awoke, I lay motionless in bed since this had always helped me in the past to remember the details of dreams. After mentally reviewing last night's dream, I reached for my dream journal on the nightstand. Since I had to help get the children ready for school and fix breakfast, I had no time to waste. I hurriedly recorded the date and started writing key words to help remember the dream's details to record later. I quickly wrote:

Marianna

African-American lady – classmate and coal miner

Coal miners' and their wives' comments

Read Amanda Literature

As I went about my morning responsibilities, I pondered the meaning of the dream. The dream symbol of the African-American woman clearly had something to do with my job problems and the Affirmative Action program. I felt disappointed. I wanted a dream to help me find a job rather than remind me about my negative attitudes associated with job-hunting.

Why was I given this dream? It bothered me that I didn't have the foggiest idea about the meaning of "Read Amanda Literature" command that I heard as I awoke from the dream. Why was the dream cloaked in obscure words and symbols when I needed a straightforward answer about getting a job?

As I served eggs to my wife, I tried to keep these thoughts about the dream from distracting me. Audrey asked, "I saw you writing in your dream journal this morning. Do you want to tell me about it?"

"I'm not sure what some of it means. It seems the first part dealt with minorities and Affirmative Action, but I'm thoroughly confused about the command given at the end of the dream."

"Maybe I can make some sense of it, if you tell it to me," she said.

Our four children were also eating breakfast at the table, and they looked up at me. It appeared they were interested in hearing it too. I paused and reluctantly began telling it.

"In the dream, I was walking from my parents' house along a street in Marianna. You know the one that goes past the old carpenter shanty building. I saw a female classmate who attended elementary and high school with me. She walked from her house to the sidewalk where I stood. I remember your family telling me that she was one of the women recently hired at the coalmine, but I don't remember anything we talked about."

"As I continued to walk down the road toward the house where you grew up, I started to remember the things I heard coal-miners and their wives saying about women who worked in the mines. Things like: It's unlucky to have a woman in the mines. They can't work like a man can. We're always doing extra work because of them. They're taking jobs from a man's family."

"At this point the dream faded away and I was in a state of twilight sleep where I couldn't see anything like I did in the visual part of the dream. I heard a male voice command me - Read Amanda Literature." I paused ... "Before going to sleep last night, I asked for guidance for a new career and where I could find a job and this is what I got."

Audrey said, "I sure hope it doesn't mean you're going to be a coal miner."

"Me too," I nodded in agreement as she continued.

"But what's that Read Amanda Literature mean?"

"I wish I knew. If I understood it, I might know more about what the dream was trying to tell me."

My youngest daughter, looked up at me from across the table with her eyes just peering over her bowl and asked, "Daddy, when are you going to get a job?"

I looked down at the floor and said, "I hope soon, honey."

***

What Does Amanda Mean?

Weeks later, I was sitting alone at the kitchen table since the children were at school and my wife was at work. I started to think about what I would cook for the family's evening meal. My thoughts wondered off and I started to fear that I might end up being a househusband for the rest of my life. I thought about being unemployed, useless, and a victim of life's cruel circumstances. My ego felt deflated as if life had thrown horse manure on me and was about to suffocate my stinky, worthless self.

I looked down at the linoleum floor and back up at the dark brown kitchen cabinets. As I aimlessly looked around, I noticed the beige wall matching the carpets. It seemed every apartment I've ever lived in was painted this same color. These drab colors deepened my depression. Will I ever get another home and paint it with colors I liked? At that point, my thoughts took an abrupt turn, and I began to wonder about Amanda Literature and its meaning.

I couldn't remember "Amanda Literature" being mentioned in any of my college or graduate school classes. In some of my infrequent meditations during this period, I asked to know the meaning of Amanda Literature, but nothing came through. I also never heard it mentioned in any of the various religious paths I had pursued. My efforts to find its meaning were fruitless.

Out of nowhere, I had a vague intuitive impression that I should use the dictionary to find the meaning of the word, Amanda. I pushed my chair back from the table and went into the bedroom to look through the unpacked boxes. After finding

101

my old college dictionary, I went back to the table and opened it to find the word Amanda.

I remembered, proper names were listed in the back part of that dictionary. When I found the word Amanda, my eyes lit up in astonishment. Amanda meant – **Worthy to Be Loved.**

The dream seemed to be telling me to love those minorities I thought were taking my jobs. They are the ones worthy to be loved.

Have you ever had a dream that helped you understand your life?

Later that evening after everyone went to bed; I sat in the living room chair and began to think about how clever divine wisdom was in coming up with the word, Amanda, as a dream symbol. It was a female name that meant worthy to be loved. It fit in perfectly with the emotional problems I struggled with concerning females now defined as minorities according to the newly legislated Affirmative Action Program. My ego consciousness was sure that this was what created the difficulties in finding a job.

The Amanda revelation did however help make me aware of the hidden resentments I had been internalizing. It informed me about my lack of love. This insight came through a backdoor via my dream since the ego mind and emotions had every other door for receiving divine guidance closed. Regardless of my admiration for this dream wisdom, it was still difficult to swallow and an even harder one to put into practice.

I realized that at a deeper unconscious level I was consumed with anger about being a victim of my employment circumstances. This anger, a mental cancer, was closing off the flow of love into and out of my heart and devouring what little love I had for others and myself.

The emotional energy of these anger cells had been increasing in strength as they consumed more and more of my heart. Any desire of mine to follow the dream's message about love was being effectively counteracted by volatile emotions. I was locked in a constant ego battle to protect what little was left of my ego's self-worth. It was a state of consciousness I did not like.

Anger Is Cancer Devouring Love & Destroying Relationships

At that time, I just didn't have the knowledge or tools to know how to allow Soul to take charge and make needed changes. The fear of financial doom, negative attitudes of self-worth, and pessimistic feelings of empowerment ruled my life. I was far from being a spiritual person, but I was about to learn one of its most valuable lessons.

I knew that learning how to control my fears and attitudes while changing anger into love would take time. My desire to cleanse my heart and to replace it with positive attitudes would be a soothing breeze of love flowing from within. If I could do this, it would open my heart to receive more love, and I would eventually be able to also give it to others.

Fill Yourself with Love to Give Love

My first task was to try to fill myself with love in order to replace the anger. I felt grateful for learning what the name Amanda meant, but I was still puzzled about what "Read Amanda Literature" meant. Did it mean to read literature worthy to be loved, like good literature? Did it mean to read literature that deals with the topic of love? Did "Amanda Literature" actually exist? Fortunately, I was about to receive additional help and insights about the full meaning of "Read Amanda Literature."

What Does "Read Amanda Literature" Mean?

During one of my meditations when I pondered the meaning of Amanda Literature, I received an intuitive nudge about the book, *Stranger by the River* by Paul Twitchell. It seemed to suggest I should read it again. I wasn't enthusiastic about that. I eventually decided to follow this inner nudge since experiences taught me that I might miss a learning opportunity. Little did I expect this nudge would help lead to one of my life's most valuable insights.

Have you ever had an inner nudge that helped give you a valuable insight?

A third of the way through the book, my consciousness was re-awakened to some of the basic principles about love that I hadn't been practicing. Love should be more than a belief or feeling. It should be demonstrated. Another principle dealt with my desire to feel loved, especially by the world outside my immediate family. If I wanted to be loved and I did, I needed to fill myself with love in order to give and receive it from others. Could this be why I was directed to read this book? The book helped focus my attention on some of the principles of love I wasn't practicing, but I still felt empty in my heart. There had to be more.

A day or two later, I read the following sentence: "So do not desire that for others which you do not desire for [yourself]..." I thought. This was what Audrey and I had been talking about concerning the dilemma of our children's desires and ours. As I continued to read, I experienced an additional insight: "Take the short cut to God and give of [yourself] ... to all." These sentences jolted my consciousness. I put the book down to reflect on its meaning.

Them versus Me Dilemma

When I was a teenager, my church taught that the ultimate expression of love was to sacrifice myself for the **good-of-others.** This was deeply embedded in my consciousness. This new idea of desiring the same for myself as for others was different. I had always thought that if I sacrificed myself for others' good, I would be practicing the highest form of love.

I knew that wanting what's good-for-others was right, but wanting what's **good-for-me** was selfishness or down right greed. Wanting something for just me was a No, No. I was always in a dilemma when I wanted something in life for myself, especially when it was in conflict with others' desires for the same thing. These experiences created inner turmoil, especially when I acted for the good-of-me. Over the years, the inner turmoil accumulated into a heavy load of guilt about being selfish. It felt as though I was carrying around a ten-ton bag of guilt.

I wondered. If I desired what's good-for-others, how would I ever get a job? Did I want others to get jobs I wanted? No, I didn't. I had a family to support. I grew up with the ego working class value that the man supported the family. Since I was unemployed, my ego's self-worth took a hard hit.

I continued thinking. I just read that I should desire the same for me that I desire for others. Was this desiring, doing what's good-for-all? If so, how was it done?

I had interpreted reality according to the beliefs and experiences of my good-for-other consciousness, but it wasn't working. I was not the one receiving the good stuff. I wondered if doing what's **good-for-all** might resolve my dilemma of them versus me. The them vs. me was how my ego differentiated itself from others. My ego viewed others as separate and used conflict to maintain this separation. In contrast, the good-for-all view was based on unity and oneness where relationships were built on love and cooperation for the greater good.

105

This new good-for-all option suggested I should desire the same good for myself as I would for others. I thought if I accepted this, I would be on an equal footing with others. If I then desired a job others wanted, I would not have to feel guilty about including myself.

I gradually understood the all, not only included others that my life touched, but the *all also included me.* At last, I did not feel I should be excluded from desiring what's good in life, and this gave me an inner freedom from the feelings of selfishness and guilt. Finally, I knew that I was to include myself as well as others when desiring something good.

Those who are deeply immersed in the ego self with its desire for the good-of-me, could easily misinterpret the meaning of the above paragraph. It is saying that the inclusion of yourself as an equal in relationships with others is what's good, but it's not suggesting an unequal desiring such as what's good-for-me. It's a difficult balance to know what good-for-all is, and we will see in a coming chapter that it takes wisdom greater than what our rational minds can grasp. That is why the good-for-all relationship requires a different approach to find a spiritual solution for life's difficulties.

Desiring and Doing What's Good-for-All Includes Me Too

About a week or so later, I was still pondering the meaning of good-for-all. It was as if I had walked into another room of my consciousness and turned on a light switch to discover there were other rooms to explore to understand love.

I knew that from then on when I wanted something in life I should desire what's *good-for-all.* This would be my main motivation in life for whatever desires or intentions I might have. Finally, I could freely and knowingly use my desires in a relationship with those who wanted the same things I did. This new realization would now serve as my new inner guidance system just like the GPS device in automobiles guided me along streets and highways.

The realization of this new value of doing and desiring what's good-for-all was a major turning point and shift in my ego consciousness.

Do you desire what's good-for-all in your life?

Arriving at this realization was a gradual process, but the application of it proved to be an even slower process. Fortunately, the "them **or** me" dilemma was resolved by desiring the good in life for them **and** me – the all.

Am I Amanda Too?

One evening as I lay awake in bed I thought, I know Audrey loves me and I love her as well as our children. I knew our children loved us though they were not pleased with the moves that resulted in lost friends. Even during times of family conflict, the children maintained kind and respectful family relationships and most of the time graciously accepted the difficulties.

Good-for-All

The ego self reacts like a robot,
Looking for the good-for-me jackpot.

Sometimes the ego works in disguise,
Sacrificing to maximize the other's prize.

Doing good-for-All is for the wise,
Equalizing and making love harmonize.

This told me that despite our differences they still loved me. They were not nomadic brats but children with loving and kind hearts. I'm proud of how my children matured in life despite the hard times they experienced. However, I knew I still had a lesson to learn about how to love myself, just as my family loved me.

I was thankful for the kindness and heartfelt love I received from my family. It provided a life jacket with enough affection to help keep my head above the negative cesspool of anger festering within, until I could eventually learn to love others and myself.

Throughout my life, the issue of loving myself bothered me. What exactly was it to love myself? Where did vanity stop and love of self begin? With only vague answers to these questions, I did know love flowed only from those who were filled with it and to be filled with love, one had to love one's self.

I knew I had to find ways to regenerate the love that my cancerous anger and fears devoured. This would help open my consciousness to allow love to flow to others, while the return flow would help replenish my own heart. This giving and receiving of love was needed to put what's good-for-all into practice.

> *Loving Yourself as Soul Fills Your Heart with Love for Others, You, and the Divine*

I eventually realized that "Amanda," which meant worthy to be loved was not only for minorities, but I was worthy of it too. If I didn't love myself, I wouldn't be able to love others. It was that simple.

I'm not sure how many years after the "Read Amanda Literature" dream that I was able to relate it to what Jesus said about love. He said, "Love your neighbor **as** yourself." He did not say love your neighbor **less than** yourself (good-for-me). He also didn't say love your neighbors **more than** yourself (good-for-others). Good-for-all love was to be given in equal portions for both oneself and others.

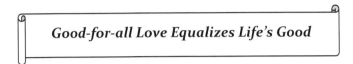

Good-for-all Love Equalizes Life's Good

It was a difficult purification process to turn the cesspool of negativity in my consciousness into loving others and myself. I had to learn to be conscious of when my thoughts were not of a loving nature and to replace them with ones in harmony with love. I also learned to live more in the presence of the Divine and its love derived from within. I took small steps to eventually fill myself with the sparkling water of pure divine love to be a channel for what's good-for-all.

I realize now that the "Amanda" dream was a turning point and was given to teach me how to be a more spiritual being of love. Since love is the greatest power in the world for peace, joy, and harmony, living a life of love will give you the power needed to be spiritual. When you intend something in your life, always desire it for the good-of-all; and when you act to realize your intentions, always do them for the good-of-all too. This is how a spiritual person lives.

Figure 7.1

**SUGGESTED QUESTIONS FOR PERSONAL
AND GROUP DISCUSSION**

1. Have you ever had an experience that taught you something about love?
2. Have you ever had a "dark night of soul" experience where you felt abandoned by the Divine and were at one of the lowest points of your life?
3. Did you learn anything from this "dark night of soul" experience?
4. Have you ever had a dream that gave you guidance?
5. Have you ever been in a dilemma about whether you should desire what's good for yourself or others?
6. Do you feel worthy to be loved?
7. How does your ego block love from being received and given?
8. Has anger ever eaten love out of your heart like a cancerous cell eats healthy cells in your body?
9. Do you fill yourself with love to be able to give love?
10. Do you mostly operate out of being good-for-me, good-for-others, or good-for-all?
11. Have you had an experience where you put good-for-all desires and actions into practice?
12. Do you want the power of love?

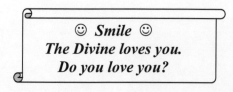

☺ *Smile* ☺
The Divine loves you.
Do you love you?

Chapter Eight

Is Win/Win the Same as Good-for-All?

When I was in a discussion group talking about the good-for-All principle, a woman asked me. "Is good-for-All like win/win in psychology?"

What do you think?

Good-for-All is similar to win/win but with an important difference. Win/win is based on conflicting relationship of winning or losing, which is part of the ego conflict state of consciousness. It uses mental judgments, logic, and reasoning of the ego self to resolve what's best for all. It tries to determine the best mental compromise for equally distributing winnings without the all-encompassing view of divine wisdom. In a win/win compromise, there is still some degree of losing, but it is better than doing what is good-for-me.

On the other hand, good-for-All is based on divine wisdom from a higher source that absolutely knows what's best for All. It derives from a consciousness of higher wisdom as well as cooperation and love. Instead of relying on ego reasoning of the mind for a solution, the Divine uses us as channels to manifest divine wisdom for the greater good. It's a higher, more compassionate, and encompassing wisdom that knows what's best for all especially when we want something that others also want. Divine wisdom knows what's good for others, me, and the divine purpose, but the ego doesn't.

> ## *Good-for-All Uses All-knowing Divine Wisdom*

***

At first, I too thought good-for-all was the same as win/win solutions. I was sincerely trying to use my rational thoughts when I searched for a new career that would be a win/win situation for my children, wife, others, employer, and to some extent myself.

After leaving my teaching position at Westminster College in 1977 and starting the accelerated nomadic life, I had a vague idea about what new career to pursue. There were two possibilities. When I worked as a carpenter in the past, I felt creative; so I thought being a construction contractor might be an interesting career. I also perceived myself as a people person and wanted to be of help to others and being a marriage, family, and child counselor was appealing too.

To qualify for either of these careers would take additional experience and education, and I wondered how I could afford to do either while still trying to support my family. In addition to the insecurity of the two career choices requiring additional skills, I was overwhelmed by financial fears. These conflicting negative thoughts and fears were not a good way to start searching for new employment. Also, my confusion about what career to pursue only confused the Divine Energy about what I intended.

Even though I intended my desires for a new career to be a win/win situation, my ego fears had taken over the decision making process. Instead of actively looking for a new career, I decided to backslide into my old career of teaching sociology or doing social research.

Choosing not to make a career change seemed more comforting than facing the fears and insecurities of learning a new one. Even this coward's way out ran into difficulties when my applications for teaching positions were counteracted by the Affirmative Action laws. In addition, when I applied for college positions in California, the newly passed Proposition 13 threatened to reduce tax funding for higher education. Consequently, California colleges were not hiring and it became a roadblock for returning to my old career. It seemed roadblocks were placed at every turn when I wanted to return to my old career. The Divine was pushing me hard to go into another career despite my fears.

While I had supported the Affirmative Action program initially, my attitude changed when I became personally affected by it. My anger increased and I felt I was a victim of reverse prejudice. I was unconsciously internalizing this victim anger, which conflicted with my beliefs about the good of affirmative action.

After a year of unemployment, I spent a summer working as a carpenter in San Diego. I wasn't making much since I was paid by piece work and I was not a fast paced carpenter, so when an opportunity opened for a college teaching position in Hazard, Kentucky, I considered it. I can remember the terrible negative feeling I had in the pit of my stomach when I signed the contract. I resisted the intuitive message of guidance and signed the contract out of financial fear. Ego fears controlled my decision.

I didn't know at the time how my ego fears were directing my life. It wasn't rational to make a lot of long distant moves as we did in a two-year span or to move without the assurance of employment or housing waiting for us. As I look back now, I can see how the fears pushed my ego buttons to behave irrational. The win/win solution was not working,

Some of the ego fears I was dealing with during the highly paced nomadic life in the latter part of 1970s were:

113

- Fear of not finding a job.
- Fear I would never know what my new career should be.
- Fear of losing what little material things we had packed in the pickup truck and trailer. During the first move to Phoenix, the trailer broke away from the truck, which is a story of a miracle to be told at another time.
- Feared the overloaded truck would not make it to the next destination. I burned out a clutch once and the mechanic said if I had the truck filled with feathers, it would have had too much weight.
- Feared I was hurting the children.
- Feared I would never own another home.
- Feared I would never gain my self-worth.
- Feared the Divine had abandoned me.
- Feared the lack of health insurance would create problems paying for the ulcer I had or any other medical bills my family would have to pay.
- Feared I would become homeless and not be able to find an apartment at the next destination that accepted four children and two dogs.

If you would ask me why we did what we did, I would have to say, my ego fears made me do it. It's similar to believing "the devil made me do it."

Have you ever seen the old TV program, "Have Gun Must Travel?" I saw a sign on an owner operated semi-truck that said, "Have Bills Must Travel." When I saw this sign while traveling in my pickup, I thought I should put a sign on my truck that read, "Have Wife, Must Travel." But I didn't.

My wife received intuitive insights especially when she did dishes, and they were usually about moving to some other place. This was what initiated many of our trips and my ego blamed her for our nomadic life. Our family should have made a rule that Mom was not allowed to do dishes, which would have saved many nomadic miles.

Figure 8.1

Now, when I look back on the nomadic life, I realize that much of her intuitive insights were good for the family, so her intuition wasn't really at fault. Many years later when I finally had nothing else to blame, I realized my ego fears were what controlled that erratic time of our life. The hard part to accept was that I was the one responsible for my own circumstances.

If I were more spiritual evolved at that time, I would have been aware of the ego reacting because of my fears. Instead of reacting, I would have accepted the situation and replaced fears with solutions of love. To do this, I would have had to allow divine love enter my state of consciousness in order to be open to good-for-All solutions. Although it took time, I feel fortunate that these negative circumstances eventually helped me become a better spiritual person.

***

Love Finds a Way while the Ego Finds Excuses

After teaching for a year in Kentucky, I tried carpentry again. When the housing market plummeted in California sometime around 1980, I was laid off. It was then that I decided to try to become a marriage, family, and child counselor. To be certified, I worked at a group home for teenagers who were having mental and emotional problems. They were not serious enough to be institutionalized in a mental hospital but had too many problems to live with their families.

***

One day at the group home, some of the staff and I were having a group counseling session with the residents. About a half-hour into the session, I heard the loud piercing sound of Divine Energy pouring through me. I had heard this familiar sound before. It was so loud that I was sure others could hear it, but there were no signs they did. I knew from experiences that this was the way the Divine used me to channel love, wisdom, or whatever was needed for others or me. I wondered who in the group was getting the benefit of this divine sound.

116

A knock on the door jolted my mind's search for an answer. The staff person told me I had a phone call in the office. When I answered the phone, it was my friend from Los Angeles. We were classmates at the University of Pittsburgh in the graduate school of sociology, and he was working at the headquarters of the Children's Home Society of California. He asked me, "Would you be interested in moving to Los Angeles and working at the headquarters as a computer systems analyst and doing some social research for my department?"

I didn't answer right away since all kinds of thoughts were going through my head. I thought, neither Audrey nor I liked living in large cities and especially Los Angeles, which is probably the gridlock capital of the world. Besides, I'm a people person and didn't want to work with impersonal computers. I also didn't know much about computers. I didn't like moving the two youngest children to another school and I didn't want to put the family through another move?

When I finally answered my friend on the other end of the line, I tried to find the right words to say, "That sounds like a good job offer, but I'm not sure how the family will feel about moving to LA. I'm also not sure I would be qualified for the job since I didn't do much computer work at Pitt or Westminster College."

"That's not a problem. We'll train you."

"That sounds good, but I will have to talk with my family and let you know."

"That's fine. I would sure like to work with you again."

"I feel the same way too."

When I talked to my wife, neither of us wanted to move to Los Angeles. The two youngest children sure didn't want to move either. As for myself, I wouldn't mind the research part of the position, but not the computer side. We initially thought that a win/win solution was to reject the job offer, but we decid-

117

ed to turn it over to the Divine to allow it to guide us. I also asked for guidance in meditation. Nothing came through except at times I would hear the presence of the inner sound as I went about my daily activities. I wondered, what was it trying to tell me? When I thought about the job, I had a good feeling inside.

These experiences were in conflict with my negative ego thoughts about the job. The ego self was reacting negatively, but the Divine guidance seemed to indicate that it was the thing to do. Fortunately, Audrey felt the same way, so we decided to accept the position even though our egos and rational thoughts were telling us otherwise. Again, the win/win mental solution wasn't the decision that the Divine was guiding us to make.

If we had continued to focus our attention on the rational mind to find a win/win solution, we would not have made a decision to take the offer. Fortunately, we turned to the Divine for guidance and we trusted that we were receiving the good-for-all solution.

***

I worked at the group home for less than a year. Eventually, I ruled out counseling as a career option just as I did carpentry, but at least I had taken the actions necessary to evaluate the two careers. The process of elimination is sometimes the way decisions are made. At least, I tried them to see if I wanted those careers.

The Divine guided me to a career that was good-for-all even though I resisted it. After the Children's Home Society of California position, I worked for Martin Marietta Aerospace Company as a financial computer systems analyst. They were responsible for building the Space Shuttle launch pad at Vandenberg AFB in California that would launch it into a north and south orbit around Earth. I also worked for Grumman Technical Services who were responsible for running and maintaining the computers that would launch the Space Shuttle.

When the first space shuttle exploded and killed all that were on board, the Shuttle program was mothballed at Vandenberg Air Force Base. After being unemployed for a while, I worked for the State of California in the Department of Corrections, Department of Justice, and the Integrated Waste Management Board as a computer systems or research analyst, which lasted until I retired.

Developing computer systems gave me a feeling of being creative. I did projects for departments that needed manual systems automated. Contrary to my belief about computer work being impersonal, I found as an analyst that most of my interactions were with people. I had to interview them to determine their needs and desires for a new computer system as well as to train them to use it. Being a computer systems analyst also used one of my strongest skills of analyzing data and information. As it turned out, it was the best career for my employers, my family, and me. That's how wise the Divine was to lead me to a career that I initially resisted.

Good-for-all wisdom from the Divine is far superior to the limited knowledge of rationally derived win/win solutions. After repeated experiences of realizing that the limitations of the ego's rational mind did not provide good-for-all guidance, I gradually turned my attention to receiving more and more guidance from the Divine in every day circumstances.

Figure 8.2

> **SUGGESTED QUESTIONS FOR PERSONAL**
> **AND GROUP DISCUSSION**
> 1. Have you tried to use win/win solutions?
> 2. Have you ever heard the inner sound of the Divine flowing through you to give guidance, peace, love, or to feel this blessing of the Divine's energy?
> 3. Have you ever made a decision to do something when your ego or rational mind said "NO," but your inner guidance said "YES?"

☺ *Smile* ☺
You do not have to find win/win solutions.
The Divine will let you know what is good-for-All.

Chapter Nine

Is Love All You Need?

After I had the "Amanda" Dream experience, I sought answers to the following questions. What is it like to live with love? Is doing what is good-for-All divine love? When am I demonstrating divine love in relationships with others? Is love all that is needed to be spiritual?

Is love doing what is good-for-all? There are various forms of love; one of them is romantic love. Most recognize this kind of emotional and sometimes blind love since the media popularizes it and it's usually the reason for marrying or divorcing someone. Even five year olds have opinions about it, which I read on the Internet.

***

Karl was asked, "What does love mean?" He said, "Love is when a girl puts on perfume and a boy puts on shaving stuff and they go out and smell each other." Leave it to children to know the essence of romantic love. I saw a TV documentary on research about how the smell of pheromones given off by males attracted females, so Karl seemed close to the truth.

***

As a teenager, I concentrated on sacrificial love (good-for-others) as taught by the church. As stated before, the "Amanda" dream became the first significant turning point in my understanding of divine love, which gradually ignited other insights.

***

For example, one evening in Boulder I was thinking about the meaning of the "Amanda" dream. I wondered, what does good-for-all really mean? I decided to do a spiritual meditation to receive an answer. Eventually, a subtle insight gently settled into my consciousness. *If you desire and do what's good-for-All, you demonstrate divine love.* It was a knowingness that came from a place deep within. I did not know how I knew it; I just knew it!

Doing Good-for-All Equals Divine Love and Vice Versa

Why hadn't I realized this before? It was such a simple truth. When I realized doing good-for-all was love, it helped make life more purposeful. I had finally solved one of my long time confusions about love. I knew now that if I desired or did something in life with all my heart for the good-of-all, I would indeed demonstrate divine love.

***

I later came to realize that the Divine also co-creates by doing what is good-for-All. Just imagine, if you remove one "o" from the word good, you have God-for-All. The Divine has an overview of a situation that humans do not. It knows all of the possible future options and the effects our intentions, motivations, or actions have on others, and it knows and does what's best for all if we desire and allow it.

I knew intentions affected others, my relationships with the Divine, and the lessons I would receive. On the other hand,

122

Divine Energy, being all-knowing, knew the specific potentials of my intentions and actions. This was why I knew I must allow the Divine to guide my intentions and actions as well as to let it co-create the what, how, when, and where of my intentions.

When I consciously co-created with the Divine, it took my desires and evaluated whether they were in harmony with the good-for-All. If they were in harmony with divine love, I would be guided to know how to help co-create it. The Divine often revises my desires and co-creates something better, or it adds a lesson or two for my spiritual development. If I allow it, the Divine always co-creates for the greater good. When I desire the good-for-All and put it into practice, I harmonize with and channel divine love.

What is the Higher Good?

In the physical world of the ego consciousness, circumstances are perceived as good or bad. It is the world of opposites. During 1977 through 1979, I was filled with fears of financial doom, unworthiness, angered about affirmative action and unemployment, victim of an uncaring world, abandoned by God, and other ego fears. I was in a downward turn of life's cycles. My ego saw no help in these situations until I realized the importance of desiring and doing what's good-for-All.

An ego's eyes never sees good in difficult circumstances. It takes a higher state of consciousness associated with living in the presence of the Divine to realize the good in difficulties, which are actually opportunities for learning love and experiencing a higher good. When I was unemployed for a year, I wondered, how could this have any good in it? I didn't realize the good in my difficulties until years later, when soul's eyes were open.

I began to understand my suffering was needed to awaken my numbed ego consciousness to the importance of doing what's good-for-All. It was one of my greatest lessons learned in life.

From the ego's perspective, it was a period filled with a lot of pain and suffering – the "baddest" of the bad cycle I ever experienced.

It is important how we perceive circumstances. The comedian, Jere Moormon defined circumstances as "Latin for the mess we're in" It is a mess according to the ego's eyes, but messes always have a potential good for learning that can help make us more spiritual.

Doing what was good-for-All became my primary motivation to make decisions based on love. The hardships I experienced were well worth the lessons gained. This wisdom helped raise my limited understanding from an ego perspective to one where I could more easily detect the good hidden within difficult circumstances. I began to realize the Divine worked behind the ego illusions and manifested what was good-for-All.

Did you notice the subtle change with the spelling of good-for-all in the above paragraphs? I capitalized the word "all," so "All" points to a more encompassing meaning than just me and another person or persons. It includes the Divine also that uses us as channels to co-create what's best for all others, all life, me, planet, as well as for the Divine's purpose and plans for our lives.

The "All" is more inclusive and puts us in harmony with the divine law of love. It is more than just what's good for the outer physical existence of humans, but it also includes what is good for inner spiritual unfoldment and the divine's purpose. Using good-for-All broadens the field of what our intentions and actions affect. It is all-inclusive and encompasses the physical as well as the spiritual dimensions.

> *Even Bad Circumstances Have a Higher Good*
> *Hidden within Them*

Desire and Do What Is Good-for-All

Co-creating is a tool for consciously changing yourself, which is motivated by love. Whenever there is something I desire or a solution is needed, I make a request of divine wisdom to let me know what will be good-for-All. I also request that my actions be done for the good-of-All. This is the purest of intentions. Only then can I open my heart and soul's eyes to the subtle messages of divine guidance and love.

> *Good-for-All Intentions Are True Spirituality*

It is my hope, your most important motivation for consciously being spiritual will be based on love rather than just for what is good-for-me or some ego based material or social success. These ego desires have their place, but they are secondary in significance to desiring for the good-of-All. This is the way you can turn ego desires for a job, loved one, car, or house into decisions of divine love. You can desire these things, but also add that you want it for the good-of-All. Desiring and doing what is good-for-All should be one's primary motivation for receiving earthly things or spiritual growth.

> *Your Action Speak Nothing Unless It Is*
> *Motivated for the Good-of-All*

Instead of using the words good-for-All, you might be more comfortable stating it in another way. For example, you could say that I want to give unconditional service to others, do God's will, walk in Jesus' footsteps, love my neighbor as myself, or do to others as I want them to do to me. You might also ask divine wisdom, what do you want me to do now? You could turn these into affirmations or inner talking as you go about your daily activities or when consciously trying to co-create something in your life.

As I said before, good-for-All served as my inner GPS guidance system and was more subtle and more difficult to follow than the woman's voice on my GPS. Even though it takes more consciousness to tune into divine guidance, it has always been a better and more direct guide for the good-of-All compared to my ego consciousness.

I also learned that when I based my inner guidance system on the good-for-All value, my life was propelled and guided with love. Since that's what I truly wanted, this goal became the cornerstone and motivation of spirituality.

Love Desires and Does What Is Good-for-All

I now have a deeper appreciation for what the "Amanda" dream meant and how pain acted as the primary motivator for learning until knowing the highest motivation of doing what's good-for-All. It established a solid foundation for me to be a co-creator and to do it with love. A higher good was subtly hidden behind the difficult circumstances I was experiencing in life. Divine love is what sets us free from ego's control, and the lessons learned were worth a zillion times the pain endured.

My realization of good-for-All was not the kind of turning point where in the next moment I became a completely different person. It has been over 30 years since I had the "Amanda" dream and the learning process is still going on. This journey made small gradual changes and will most likely be a life-long marathon without a finish line in sight. I have heard that the Divine works slowly, but when it comes to my spiritual growth, I've been moving at a sloth's pace for most of my life until recently.

LOVE SETS YOU FREE

Choices have consequences you must agree,
  Making Life's circumstances what they will be.

Ego fears, habits, and jealousies,
  Limits freedom like electronic devices on parolees.

While love's the key that sets you free,
  It's how Divine trainees receive graduate degrees.

The significance of my shifts in consciousness went almost unnoticed until later in life. It was like walking on a moonlit beach and not being aware of the slow rising tide until I felt it between my toes. Important realizations tend to sneak subtly into my consciousness rather than by earth-shaking experiences or blowing trumpets.

All You Need Is Love

The Divine Source is the origin of divine love, and our purpose in life is to use it to co-create for the greater good. Divine Energy is divine love flowing from the Divine Source. When we live in divine presence, we receive messages of guidance and feel divine love as a heightened feeling of inner joy and peace. Divine love can also be experienced in the form of inner light and sound. If you see the inner light or hear the sound, this is divine love too.

Have you ever experienced the inner light or sound?

The light that blinded St. Paul on the road to Damascus filled his heart with love for Christians rather than the hatred he once had for them. Experiencing these divine manifestations lets you know the Divine is using you as a channel for divine love. This is not the only way divine love appeared or operated in my life, which will be discussed more fully in another book. For love to manifest on the outer, we must consciously choose it and demonstrate it with actions.

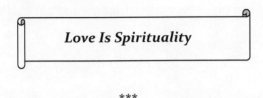

Love Is Spirituality

***

We sometimes receive the Divine's love spontaneously as my wife did. One evening in 1969 or 1970 Audrey was watching Billy Graham on television, she felt disturbed about his message of us being sinners, needing forgiveness, and in need of salvation. She said, "Please God, help me to know the truth." In an instant, she transcended her physical existence to experience the love, peace, and joy of the Divine that surpassed all understanding. All she could say to describe it in words was to say, "I felt the love of God."

***

The truth is that the Divine is not wrathful or to be feared, and we are not sinners needing to feel guilty because Jesus was crucified some 2,000 years ago. This was a church dogma added long after Jesus death to try to make sense of why the son of God was killed as a young man and in such a cruel way. The truth is that the Divine is love and we are to love the Divine, the Divine in us as Soul, and to love others even our enemies. Love is all you need.

I'm realizing more and more that love is at the root of all I should do in life. Love others. Love my work. Love family. Love animals. Love God. Love myself. Love life. Love nature. Love all things. It's like the Beatles' song, "All You Need Is Love." Life's main purpose boils down to this. I've found the major lesson is learning love from life's difficulties. Consequently, it has become my primary purpose and motivation for being spiritual.

Jesus and Love

When I was a teenager, I was introduced to Jesus' teachings of love though I didn't see his teachings practiced much by church members. I also didn't understand much about how to put his love into practice. I always thought it was doing what was good-for-others (sacrificial love). It took me about another 24 years to have my next major understanding, which was initiated by the "Amanda" dream.

The ironical part of all of this was that Jesus taught what divine love and good-for-All were when I was a teenager, but it took years to understand his gift. I went through a lot of hard knocks and pain to eventually make a full circle back to understand what Jesus taught.

There were three basic teachings of Jesus that are the basis for what I call divine love:

- *"Love the Lord your God with all your heart ... soul, and ... mind. This is the greatest and first commandment."* By loving the Divine, your heart opens to divine love and fills you with it. When I desired something to be for the good-of-All, I am filled with love for the Divine. Otherwise, I would have been trying to get pure water out of an empty bottle. Don't forget that loving yourself as Soul is love of the Divine.

  Do you love the Divine?

> ***Love Is the Oil That Runs Life Smoothly***
> ***And the Glue Uniting Us in Peace & Harmony***

- *"You shall love your neighbor as yourself."* This is the best example of good-for-All love rather than

129

the good-for-other love the church taught me. It's loving everything equally.

Do you love yourself as well as your neighbor?

- *"You have heard that it is said, 'You shall love your neighbor and hate your enemies.' But I say to you, love your enemies ...."* Wow! If you want your love to be for the good-of-All, just include your enemies. This is the part of the "All" that most people do not want to include in the practice of love.

Do you love those that intend to harm you or disagree with you?

If You Love Your Enemies, You'll Have No Enemies

Love establishes a firm foundation for spirituality. Co-creating with love will improve not only your individual state of consciousness and life, but it will also help change the collective consciousness. The next chapters will discuss the shift from ego-empowerment to spiritual-realizations.

Figure 9.3

**SUGGESTED QUESTIONS FOR PERSONAL
AND GROUP DISCUSSION**

1. Have you ever had an experience where you did something for the good-of-All and felt the love?
2. Can you remember an experience where the ego saw only bad in a situation but later you realized a lesson, understanding, or something positive resulted from a difficulty?
3. Have you ever experienced how divine wisdom guides you to do what was best for All?
4. At what pace has your spiritual growth been progressing? (Snails? Walking? Jogging? Or Running?)
5. Would you agree that "All You Need Is Love?"

☺ *Smile* ☺
All you need is love.
Are you filled with love so you can give it?

SHIFT IV

Ego-Empowerment to Spirituality

What are the major signposts on the journey of being spiritual? This question can also be asked as, what are the shifts in consciousness needed to be spiritual? Spirituality can progress through the phases of ego-empowerment, which includes me-empowerment, other-empowerment, and ego-realization. You may have already progressed beyond these phases of being spiritual and on the journey of spiritual-realization. This is where spirituality progress from Soul-realization, to co-realization, and to Divine-realization.

It doesn't matter at what point you find yourself on the journey; you are spiritual when you sincerely have that intention. The most important thing you need to do to be more spiritual is to start moving your spiritual consciousness forward to increase your energy vibrations of love and to be more and more in charge of the ego. As you heighten your spirituality you make a blessed life for yourself as well as increase the probability of the Love Age happening where peace, freedom, happiness, and love fill the world. You should also know that spirituality is a journey without a finish line.

Chapter Ten

Ego-empowerment Journey

The ego consciousness has basic ways it empowers its life. Some use being a victim to control others or their circumstances, or they try to manipulate the random forces of chance or luck. Others use complaining, anger, greed, or even violence to obtain their selfish desires. I refer to this phase as me-empowerment, which has the motivating force of getting what is good-for-me.

As the spiritual journey progresses, some transition into the other-empowerment phase where they try to bring social justice, equality, world peace, feeding and healing the poor, and saving animals or the environment. In this phase doing what's good-for- others is the motivating force.

The turning point during the ego-empowerment stages is when you reach ego-realization. This is the point where you become aware how your ego habits control your life. At this point, it is usually a mental awareness of the unproductive nature of ego habits as well as the pain it creates. Once you reach this awareness, you're on your way to really doing something about being spiritual.

Figure 10.1 is an illustration of the ego-empowerment stages that you may go through or have already experienced. Although these are ego stages as you progress from the me-empowerment to ego-realization stage, you are growing spiritually. You may start life at the other-empowerment or ego-realization stages or even at a higher stage.

As I look back over where my journey has taken me, I've wondered how I moved from the ego consciousness to being able to empower myself with love. Since I'm writing a book about the journey, I tried to make sense of it by constructing stages of consciousness that I went through. Many of you will travel through the stages I experienced, but yours will be unique for you. These stages tend to be a progression of experiences, which many people will probably travel through on their spiritual journey while others start at higher vibrational levels. Use them as a relative representation of what your spiritual journey may be like.

I do not know much about Eckhart Tolle's life, but he seemed to have shifted his consciousness from either the me-empowerment or the other-empowerment stages to the Divine-realization stage in one night, which is the peak level of spirituality. The first two years after his experience, he lived on a park bench probably interpreting his experiences and learning to balance his new spiritual consciousness with the experience of living in the material and social worlds.

You should not limit your journey to having to go through all of the stages I have provided in this chapter or the next one. It is very unusual to progress as fast as Eckhart Tolle did, and most of you will probably mature spiritually at a slower pace by taking smaller steps as I did. Fortunately, there are signs that the pace of spirituality is increasing since the spiritual collective consciousness has heightened its spiritual vibrations. This helps all of us.

As a Divine Self you are already spiritual. You just have to

Figure 10.1

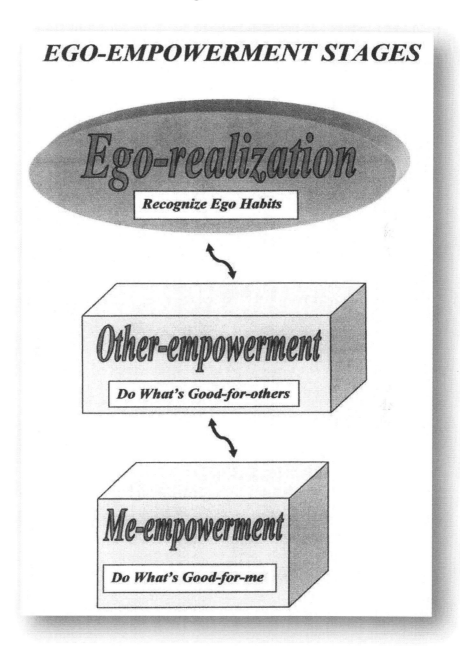

realize what you already are as Soul. Soul is already at the peak of spirituality and your journey is to realize it.

> ## Usually Spiritual Journeys Happen by Small Steps rather than One Big Leap

As the ego and spiritual stages are discussed, you might want to examine your own life and decide where you're experiencing place you. This could help you recognize where you are in your spiritual growth or state of realization and what to focus on for moving consciousness forward to a higher level of spirituality.

Me-empowerment

In some way or another, anyone who is in the me-empowerment stage considers themselves a victim. Many view themselves as victims of others, their life's circumstances, or the random forces of luck, chance, and God's wrath. Sometimes, these people do strange things to influence the roll of life's dice. My grandmother for example had a strange way of creating good luck for bingo.

***

When I was eight or nine years old, my mother, brothers, and I visited my grandparent's apartment. I stood next to my mother in the kitchen listening to her talk to grandma who was sitting on a maroon cushion that looked too large for a kitchen chair. I asked, "Why is your cushion so big, grandma?"

"It's filled with horse manure. I'm sitting on it, so I'll have good luck for bingo tonight."

"Are you going to take it to bingo?"

"Sure am. It's going to win me a lot of money."

"How did you get manure in it? Wasn't it sloppy and stinky?"

"It's dried manure, honey; but you have to make sure its horse manure and not from cows. I wrapped it good. Put padding over it and sewed on the cover. I know another woman who does this, and she's always lucky at bingo."

***

I didn't say any more, but I thought to myself, I'd never do that to get good luck. By the way, I had never observed any improvement in her financial status, so you might not want to try a horse manure pillow for good luck.

Me-empowerment is the main mode how most people relate to others and their environments. For the first four decades of my life, I viewed luck as the primary determinant, much as it was for my grandmother. It seemed as though I was in a conflict with the universe to minimize bad luck. To avoid bad luck, I practiced some superstitions such as hanging a rabbit's foot on my belt loop, not opening umbrellas in the house, or not walking under a ladder. However, I didn't take it to the extent of doing the kinds of things my grandmother did.

I sort of resigned myself to the universe's luck and felt little or no responsibility for creating life's destiny. Luck disempowered me. I felt powerless and a victim of luck and chance, which left me with little control over life's direction. I was at the mercy of the unpredictable winds that blew me around like a leaf into unwanted circumstances and consequences.

> **If You Think Life's Created by Luck and Chance,**
> **You'll Live in a Powerless Trance**

139

Added God's Wrath to Victim Consciousness

As a teenage member of the Methodist church, I learned the importance of fearing God's wrath as another of those uncertain universal forces. God's wrath was similar to bad luck since it came at unexpected times and I wasn't sure why I was experiencing it. I also learned that when something went wrong, it was God's will, which was a softer version of God's wrath. As a youth, I viewed God's wrath and/or luck as the basic forces creating my destiny.

***

When my cousin died as a child, I learned from the church that her death was God's will. I wondered why God did such mean things to children and feared God might do it to me someday. Now, I view children's deaths as part of a spiritual plan they established on the inner before birth, which usually serves as a gift for parents or others to gain spiritual understanding. When my cousin died, her parents turned to religion and as far as I could tell, it made advancements in their spiritual understanding. One of her sisters made a great deal of spiritual advancement, but I'm not sure how much of it was related to her sister's death. As I see it, my cousin's death was a gift to her family.

> *Most Believe Luck and God's Wrath*
> *Are Negative Forces Affecting Destiny*

In another experience in 2010 where a parent was dealing with death of a young adult son, I saw the lack of understanding of this gift and how a parent took refuge in the victim consciousness. The parent was a contractor who was remodeling my home and we talked about his son's death. He was swimming in the victimization of grief and was having a difficult time keeping his business going. He was fortunate that one of his workers kept it operating.

We all have a choice of accepting the gift of a child's death, disability, or any other difficulty for our or their spiritual maturity. This may sound cruel, but it was something the child and parents' Souls agreed to on the inner before their child's birth. In families, we are truly co-planners helping each other experience lessons for the unfoldment of spiritual consciousness. This is why family members tend to keep reincarnating over and over in the same extended family. Those under ego's victim consciousness have a very difficult time accepting these difficulties as gifts for learning.

Have you ever had to make a choice about how to handle a family or friend's death or other kind of loss?

Additional Victim Forces

During this phase of my life, I felt I had some power by controlling others. One way that I did it was to make others feel sorry for me as a "poor victim" of the universe. If they felt sorry for me, they would do something to help me. I became aware of this ego habit during the time I was in college, but it took me years to minimize the use of it.

A more powerful force I used to control others was complaining. I judged and blamed others for their inappropriate behavior in order to control them to do what I wanted. I was also protecting my ego since things happening in my life were never viewed as my responsibility. My problems stemmed from the faults of others or some outside forces that victimized me.

The ego lives in conflict to empower and protect itself as well as to control others. Its motivation is to get what is good-for-me. In order to do this, its primary way of empowerment is using emotional force or at times even resorting to physical violence.

The victim consciousness uses guilt to make others feel sorry for them, which manipulates others to get what is good-for-me. Some of the other emotional tactics for manipulating others are anger, jealousy, gossip, fears, lies, shame, criticism, diminish another's self-worth, threats, prejudice, and intolerance to name a few.

As a college student, I learned that God's wrath and luck were not the only external factors affecting me. When I studied sociology in college; I began to wonder how much my parent's socialization, society's uncaring institutions, culture, or poor genetic inheritance determined my life. These factors became additional external forces contributing to my disempowerment.

The masses of humanity are in a victim state of disempowerment as I was for about the first 40 years or more of life. The ego consciousness lives in a state of disempowerment. Also, oppressive governments, parents, cultures, political ideologies, religious dogma and rituals, commercial ads, and other social controls contribute to the victim state of consciousness. Spiritual people do not let people or institutions with military boots march through their minds and emotions. Control your own life with the loving assistance of the Divine.

> *Beware of Military Boots Marching Through Your Mind*

Power of an Empty Feeling

In addition to eventually realizing that difficulties were lessons for me to learn from, there are other ways the Divine helped me during the me-empowerment phase. My parents never attended church when I was a child, but they were good moral people. When I became a teenager, I had an inner feeling of emptiness about my parent's life. As I look back on this experience, it must have been Soul's dissatisfaction prompting me to search for a solution. My inner feeling of emptiness pushed me to grow spiritual. This emptiness was a power that motivated me toward spirituality, but I was not aware of it at the time. It helped motivate me to do things to grow spiritual such as to take the step to attend church.

Roger Walsh in his book *Essential Spirituality* referred to this emptiness as "divine discontent." This uneasy inner feeling of emptiness served to push me up higher rungs of my destiny's spiritual ladder. I didn't realize it at the time, but this divine uneasiness was a source of inner guidance and wisdom telling me it's time to move on to something else. Fortunately, this empowerment tool was available during the time I was under the control of the ego consciousness, but I was unconscious of the help I was receiving.

> ### *Feelings of Emptiness Are Inner Sources of Guidance*

Have you ever felt divine discontent or a sense of emptiness pushing you forward spiritually?

Another source of guidance is when one's mental awareness begins to realize the pain ego habits are causing, and the mind begins to seek solutions. Eventually, I realized that the good-for-me value of the ego does not create the harmony and happiness in relationships I desired. The turning point for this stage occurred when I was in college and decided to open my heart to other's good through non-violent changes.

Other-empowerment

The choice that helped me transition into the other-empowerment state of consciousness derived from the decision to attend college where the illumination of the mind broadened my perspective beyond fundamental Christianity. As I look back on the decision to attend college, it was set up by outside forces. I told this story in an earlier chapter that had the Divine Spirit's fingerprints all over it. Sometimes, the Divine pushed me into situations by setting up circumstances that shoved me one way or the other. It contributed to my spiritual destiny by blocking my path to being a coal miner since the mines had laid off miners. This was another way the Divine helped guide me early in life when I was still in an unconscious ego state.

Destiny Is Not Predestined;
It's the Cumulative Result of Your Choices

My mind was a double-edged sword where it created my ego consciousness into hardened habits that were difficult to change. On the other edge were the mental abilities for analyzing, recognizing the problems of ego habits, and realizing the habits needed changed. My college education started to bring out the powers of the mind to initiate changes in my life and to open me to alternative spiritual paths.

Social Empowerment in Religion and Science

At West Virginia Wesleyan College, I transitioned into the other-empowerment consciousness and made a shift from faith-based religion to social religion and evidence-based science. The driving force behind these changes related to choosing a liberal interpretation of the Bible, selecting sociology as a major, and living a non-violent life. I was shifting from faith-based to evidence-based knowing and wanted to change the world to be a more peaceful and just place to live.

These choices moved the other-empowerment phase of my life into high gear where I believed the powers of non-violence and the knowledge of sociology could help create a better social environment here on Earth. This spirituality became more important than the desire for salvation and going to heaven, which tended to be for the good-of-me. I was now moving into the consciousness of what's good-for-others, which is a higher stage of spiritual consciousness.

Chose liberal Christianity. I shared in an earlier chapter an experience of the New Testament class at West Virginia

Wesleyan College where I moved from a fundamentalist interpretation of the Bible to a liberal one based on evidence. It was a significant choice that helped me move from a faith-based to an observational or evidence-based consciousness.

I was beginning to rely on the importance of observations instead of faith-based reliance on religious dogma, secondhand knowledge, and myths. This helped open my mind to focus on changing the social environment as well as creating more social justice and world peace. This was a turning point that opened my heart to help others.

Chose Non-violence. I left the Methodist church since I had a deep feeling of emptiness when attending worship services and felt alienated from God. During this time I struggled with my blind-faith in the Bible. I was also struggling with the question of how to relate to what was going on in the early 1960's, with the civil rights and peace movements. I was shifting my religious consciousness toward social religion where I became more concerned about establishing heavenly peace, justice, and love here on Earth.

After reading a book by Mahatma Gandhi, I was committed to a non-violent life. Non-violence was a moral and collective way to change society's institutions to make them more peaceful and just. I couldn't understand why the Methodist church did not see the importance of Jesus' teaching about turning the other cheek. Non-violence was an element of Jesus' teaching of love.

Jesus was also a social activist and supported those treated unjustly during his times. The synagogues and temples did not allow the sick, poor, and prostitutes to attend services. They hated Samaritans and treated them unfairly. Jesus taught tolerance and loving everyone. Loving one another was his approach to life even when it came to an enemy. I wondered, why wasn't the church teaching and doing more about today's injustices? Why weren't they more interested in world peace rather than justifying wars?

145

My belief in non-violence as a moral power grew, and I realized it could help make groups a powerful agent for changing social institutions. It gave me an opportunity to take an active role with others in creation rather than standing back and letting God or luck do it. It was a source of social empowerment, and I was becoming more conscious of the importance of joining with others to use non-violence as a source of empowerment.

> ## Other-empowerment Is a Collective Way to Change Social Institutions

Sociology and social change. At the same time I was going through this transition in religious consciousness, I was in the process of deciding what my college major would be. I decided to major in sociology, which was another choice for evidence-based knowing by means of the scientific method.

When I studied sociology at West Virginia Wesleyan College, I believed it would lead to a more reliable source of information about social behavior and how to do peaceful social change. Since it used first-hand observations and scientific methodologies, sociology was evidence-based using research to control the personal biases of the scientist and capturing the actual reality of observed social behavior. In addition, other scientist could duplicate the research to recheck the reality of a study's conclusions. Scientific methods used rigorous means to check the validity of its data.

I wanted to use sociology to further my scientific understanding of social change as well as non-violence to make a better world. I hoped to combine these two to create a world where social and racial justice as well as world peace would thrive. I even pursued a doctor's degree in the field of sociology at the University of Pittsburgh with this motivation in mind.

As much as possible, I wanted my beliefs to be based on objective evidence and verifiable experiences. I didn't want faith to be my final validation for what I believed. I saw faith as a starting point rather than an end for knowing until I could find more objective or experiential source of information to support or not support what I believed. Later in life, I eventually understood another aspect of the faith that Jesus wanted used. Rather than using it to believe in church dogma or beliefs, faith was a way for me to move mountains or change myself. Unfortunately, at that time I felt I only had the power to move molehills.

Non-violence and sociology gave me a sense of other-empowerment. I felt I was taking steps toward understand the world more objectively and that would help to make it more peacefully. However, I became no more than a non-violent theorist or idealist rather than a non-violent activist.

Even though I viewed social life as being possible to change, sociology caught me in another web where I realized there were additional social factors controlling my life. It helped expanded my victim state of consciousness to an extent. Sociology was like a double edge sword that gave me the hope of understanding social change, but at the same time making me realize that the social environment was the primary causes of my ego behavior.

Emptiness of Quakers and non-violence. I joined a Quaker meeting in Salem, Ohio after graduating from West Virginian Wesleyan College and accepting an English and social studies teaching position at Leetonia High School. Since Quakers believed in non-violence, I became a member of this group to associate with like-minded believers. I was not much of an activist and did not get involved in non-violent protests, but my heart supported the peace movement during the Vietnam War and the racial and social justice changes of the 1960s and 1970s. I believed my primary role was to understand violence, non-violence, and social change from a scientific perspective to contribute information to help create a more peaceful and just world.

I was impressed with the earlier Quaker leaders such as George Fox who used the experiences of the "Inner Light" or the

147

"Christ within" to find inner peace. This was what their non-violence beliefs and practices evolved from. They started out as a mystical Christian group.

***

At the first Quaker meeting I attended in Ohio, one of the members asked me, "How did you find out about Quakers?"

"I read about George Fox and the early Quakers in college since I was interested in non-violence. I was very impressed with their ability to experience the "Inner Light.""

"Well, we're not like that anymore...."

I didn't fully understand his response, but after a year I realized that seeking the guidance of the "Inner Light" to find a deep sense of inner peace was no longer practiced by most Quakers. The early Quakers used the silent meetings to experience the "Inner Light," which created a state of inner peace and motivated desires for outer peace.

Modern day Quakers were different. A Quaker in Pittsburgh told me that the meetings were more like an academic popcorn machine where one Quaker gave a rational talk followed by others popping up to give their academic or rational responses or rebuttals. The Pittsburgh Quaker meeting relied on reasoning and the mind rather than inner spiritual experiences of peace.

I became disillusioned with the Quakers and non-violence as a way to change the world. I'm not suggesting that society cannot be changed by non-violent methods since Gandhi and Martin Luther King's nonviolence are proof that it can be done.

> ### *Non-violence Is a Moral Means of Other-empowerment*

When I joined the Quakers, I desired non-violence, but when I left the Quakers I was more interested in experiencing the "Inner Light" and the inner peace it brought. It started my search for establishing a direct relationship with the Divine rather than the outer religious dogmas and secondhand experiences handed down by churches.

The main consciousness change during the other-empowerment stage was to widen my heart to help others solve the world's social problems. It was the same kind of movement that is happening in Christianity today. The book by Rick Warren, *The Purpose Driven Life*, and his world-wide programs to help with hunger, health, and other problems is an example of other-empowerment in action.

Others who go through this stage do not get involved in religious organization, but join all types of humanitarian, environmental, and animal right's programs to make the world a better place to live for all life. This stage helps broaden the heart to include larger groups of life and a concern for the good-of-others.

Emptiness of Sociology

When I was teaching at Westminster College in the mid-1970s and working on my Ph. D., I started to feel an inner emptiness and disillusionment with sociology and its possible contributions to non-violence and helping to create a better world. I expected the social sciences to contribute to the understanding of non-violent change and world peace, but their power to solve these problems was more like a flashlight with dead batteries. Sociology and most of the other human sciences were focused on the ego, while my spiritual experiences were telling

149

me that the ego was the primary causes of my unproductive be-haviors.

I became disillusioned with sociology and my heart was no longer interested in teaching it. I eventually decided to stop working on my Ph. D. at the University of Pittsburgh, which was a condition for continued employment at Westminster College and receiving tenure. I knew this decision meant I would have to leave college teaching. My previous ego search for personal happiness in a career went up in fumes.

I didn't know what career would satisfy my emptiness, it was a confusing and difficult time. When I tried being a carpenter and a marriage, family, and child counselor, I experienced emptiness again. The pushing force of spirit moved me toward other options. Finally, I chose to be a computer system analyst, and my empty feeling about a career was satisfied until I decided to retire at 59 to write this book.

I was also embroiled in other turmoil. Who am I and what's the meaning of life? This was the period right before the turning point of the "Amanda Dream" experience. With all this turmoil in my life, I was beginning to move from the other-empowerment stage to look for other answers.

Have you ever experienced wanting to make the world a better place to live and later became disillusioned with it?

Push and Pull Forces Affecting Destiny

If you noticed the me-empowerment and other-empowerment phases of my life, the Divine tended to be the primary forces pushing me in different directions. This happened due to the unconscious nature of my ego consciousness where the Divine and the pain of karma nudge me into situations that would help fulfill my spiritual plan. Inner feelings of emptiness, uneasiness, circumstances blocking my desires, and new opportunities opening up pushed me away from old worn out religious paths, careers, or other aspect of life.

These feelings tended to happen before major changes in my life and served as difficulties, new opportunities, and feelings of emptiness that motivated me to move forward. However, I was always the one who had to make the final decision about the forces that were pushing me. Pulling forces, such as using conscious intentions, were more important later in affecting the direction of my spiritual destiny.

Ego-realization Stage

Early in the 1970s, I found myself working on controlling my emotional habits such as anger, trust, and other unproductive ego reactions. I knew I had to gain mental control over my emotional habits and their tendency to cause wide swings in my emotions. It wasn't until the early 1990s when I recognized my most serious ego habit of complaining and decided to do something about it.

I discussed in a previous chapter how my wife and I became aware of our complaining/guilt relationship and how we tried to solve it with the mind. When I eventually recognized the deeper levels of fear that underlie my ego reactions, I gained a deeper understanding of the workings of the ego. We tried unsuccessfully to tell each other when we noticed the other using guilt or complaints. The mental solution at times stirred up more ego reactions than stopping the disharmony.

It's futile to try to correct another's ego problems since it will most likely ignite an ego war. Since you can only change yourself, just focus on replacing your own ego habits with spiritual ones. Be patient, most spiritual pioneers evolve over time by replacing one ego habit at a time. This will most likely be the predominant way of change for the Love Age.

What is one way your ego brings conflicts and unhappiness into your life?

To a degree, the mind can control one's emotions. Back in the 1970s, I began to gain some control over the broad swings in my emotions, but this also was a work in progress over time. Ego-realization starts with the mind recognizing its unproductive habits, then controlling the emotional reactions.

An ego-realized person understands that the ego mind and its habits are detrimental to peace, happiness, and love. When one also realizes that the world of the human ego and matter are built on nothing more than mental illusions, ego realization increases.

The ego-realization stage was primarily recognition of my ego habits, how fear ignited them, and how they controlled my unconscious emotional reactions that created a life of conflict and pain. The mind's power of analysis and observation started to control my emotional responses, but I gradually realized there was a limitation to the mind's control over ego's reactions.

I started to transition from the ego-realization stage when I had an awareness of most of my ego habits and their related fears. The nail in the coffin was at a higher spiritual realization when I gained a degree of soul awareness that could recognize, control, and stop the ego's reaction at its initial point of reaction to difficulties. For a while, I felt straddled between the world of the ego and spirit, but this started to cease when I transitioned into the next stages of spiritual-realization.

Are you ego-realized?

The ego and the mind that were the primary sources of empowerment during the ego-empowerment stages were viewed as being too limited to carry me any further along my spiritual journey. I had to make a major shift from the mental and social sources of power to a consciousness where love became the source of power. This was the point where being spiritual really started to use its powers to change the ego. This will be the discussion for the next chapter of the spiritual-realization stages.

Figure 10.2

SUGGESTED QUESTIONS FOR PERSONAL AND GROUP DISCUSSION

1. Are you aware that you have a spiritual plan for your life?
2. Are you operating in the me-empowerment, other-empowerment, or ego-realization phase?
3. Have you ever felt you were a victim of chance, luck, or God's wrath?
4. Have you had a significant person or helper to keep you moving forward with your spirituality?
5. Is luck, chance, or God's wrath a primary factor determining your life?
6. Are you using mental and emotional ego habits to control others?
7. Have you ever had a feeling of emptiness about life that helped push you forward in you spiritual growth?
8. Have you ever experienced a death or difficulty in life that you now see as a gift for spiritual growth?
9. Do you let people march through your mind and emotions with military boots?
10. Have you ever been part of the other-empowerment consciousness?
11. Have you ever made a decision that the mind had serious limitations in helping you to be a more spiritual person?
12. Are you ego-realized?

☺ *Smile* ☺
Ego-realization is recognizing ego habits.
That's a significant spiritual step in being spiritual.

Chapter Eleven

Spiritual-realization Journey

When my mother was 91 years old, she told me a joke about an older lady named Rose. Rose attended church faithfully and tried her best to understand Pastor Tim's sermons. One Sunday morning, Pastor Tim's spoke about the "Hereafter." He encouraged his flock to place their attention on the 'Hereafter" for this is the realm of spirit and God.

After the service was over, Pastor Tim stood at the front door greeting his parishioners as they left church. When Rose approached the Pastor, she said, "You know the older I get, the more I think about the hereafter." Pastor Tim reached out to shake her hand while saying, "Rose, I'm so thankful to here you say that."

Rose then put her hand on her chin as though she was pondering something and said, "Almost every time I go down to my basement, I'm always asking myself; what am I here after?"

Most people in their ego consciousness are as confused about where their attention should be focused as Rose was. Their ego eyes focus only on the realities of the physical and mental worlds. Those that are spiritual and using the eyes of Soul know they must view the reality of both the physical and spiritual worlds. The spiritual powers that rely on the wisdom and love from the "Hereafter" will begin to be realized.

Spiritual-realization Stages

To have spiritual-realization, attention needs refocused from the material world or ego consciousness to the world of spirit where Soul and the Divine have the powers to transform life with love. Tapping into the power of Soul is a major transition where Soul controls the mind, emotions, and imagination and operates in a co-creative partnership with the Divine and others.

The transition between the material and spirit worlds is subtle and difficult to know what is going on at times. It is also more difficult to define clear-cut stages. Ego-empowerment tends to be more linear where you progress from me-empowerment to other-empowerment and on to ego-realization. Spiritual-realization on the other hand tends to be more of a feedback or circular model of progress. I have found it more difficult to know where I fit into the stages of spiritual-realizations than it was for ego-empowerment.

I have found that there is a strong interconnection between being Soul-realized and Co-realized. It seemed they almost progressed at the same time and greatly depended on each other for further spiritual growth as well as for ego-realization.

Eastern religions and mystical groups of various religions have defined spiritual stages in terms of realizations. I'll use these categories with modifications to help define the stages one might go through to be more spiritual. See Figure 11.1 for an

Figure 11.1

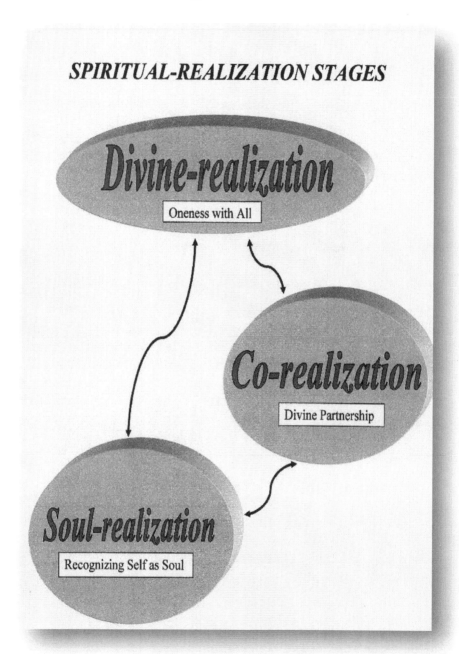

illustration of the spiritual-realization stages of Soul-realization, co-realization, and Divine-realization.

Transition between Ego-empowerment and Spiritual-Realizations

In the ego state of consciousness, humans are unconscious operators and as they make the transition between the human and spirit worlds, they become semi-conscious and eventually live in full Soul consciousness. The mind and its social constructed illusions are in control before the transition into spiritual-realizations, but as Soul increases in power, it eventually controls the mind, emotions, and imagination. As you become a more realized being, you serve as a clearer channel for the Divine's love, wisdom, and know your part in the divine's plan.

The infrequent experiences I initially had of the spiritual consciousness made me feel trapped in the unwanted human consciousness of the ego. Physical eyes cannot see into the spiritual worlds. At times, I felt like I was in sort of a no-man's land. As I progressed in spiritual understanding and experiences, I began to feel more and more part of the spiritual worlds. My spiritual eyes observed life from a high spiritual perspective rather than from ego's eyes looking up from the gutters of the material world.

Trying to determine exactly when I transitioned from one stage to another was not clear. Sometimes, aspects of spiritual-realization stages were mentally realized while operating in the ego consciousness. I believed mentally that I was Soul long before I could operate to some degree as a soul-realized being.

The same process occurred with love. When I had the "Amanda Dream," I gained a mental understanding of divine love, but I did not experience it from within until later in life. Most often, the stages started as a mental understanding and over time, they slowly became a conscious experience of Soul and a way of life.

Psychics and Edgar Casey

In 1970 or 1971 Audrey became a truth seeker when she had an experience of feeling the love of the Divine. She broadened her reading of books about psychics who predicted things about the future and discussed other spiritual subjects.

I was a professor at Westminster College during that time. I was mainly rooted in the ego consciousness of the past and the possibilities of the future. My commitment to scientific reasoning could not accept someone predicting the future. It just wasn't scientifically possible. Eventually, after being shown examples of psychics that did it, my hardened attachments to old beliefs began to crack.

Audrey became interested in Edgar Casey. After hearing how he could receive information derived from the spiritual worlds to heal people while in trances, I began to realize that valid information could be obtained from other sources than science. I could obtain divine wisdom from the spiritual realms.

Casey also shared information about the death and rebirth process. I had already given up on the Heaven and Hell dogma that I was taught in church since no loving God would ever place one of his children in a state of Hell for eternity. May be a wrathful God would. An ordinary earthly father who loved his child would not even do that.

Reincarnation and karma were much more than just being shoved into Hell for wrong beliefs or actions. Casey helped me believe I had many lives to learn lessons from the consequences of my ego's consequences or karma. It made me realize that life had purpose and I wasn't living as a victim of luck or God's wrath. I was the cause of my circumstances and responsible for changing them. This freed my victim consciousness to be

159

responsible and to use its powers to help change my life to be more spiritual.

Have you ever been a seeker of truth?

Chose Eckankar™

I had already left the Quakers because of a feeling of an inner emptiness there. I felt they lacked a direct connection with the Divine's inner peace, which should have been the motivation for non-violent beliefs and actions. After two or three years of reading about Edgar Casey and being in one of his groups in Hendersonville, North Carolina, Audrey and I felt we received all we could from Casey, and the feeling of spiritual emptiness came back. I was tired of hearing and reading about others who were having inner spiritual experiences. I wanted to have them myself.

In 1971, a member of our Edgar Casey study group received an announcement that Eckankar™, The Science of Soul Travel was going to have a discussion group in Ashville. Some of us decided to investigate what it and soul travel were all about. After reading one book and attending a meeting, Audrey and I decided to buy the discourses that allowed us to join the discussion group. At this point, we were both making a decision to move on with our spiritual life. I felt it might help me have those inner spiritual experiences I had desired since being a Quaker.

Eckankar™ used meditation to project out of the body to experience inner spiritual worlds. After years of meditation, I never had an experience where I travelled and observed places or entities in the spiritual worlds. I did have experiences mainly at seminars where I would experience the inner light of God, which was a manifestation of Divine Energy. Much later, I came to experience the inner sound of God in meditation, but it mainly came while I was engaged in everyday activities. At first, it was an intermittent experience and took some 25 years to establish a more frequent daily connection with the divine's light and sound. The reason it took so long was that I had difficulty quieting the mind to experience the divine's presence and I had my goals set on projecting from the body rather than experiencing the stillness of the Divine.

During this time, I also used the mind to learn some of the self-help empowerment techniques for empowering life. I was introduced to setting goals, saying affirmations, and visualizing. These mental, emotional, and imaginative powers helped me direct my life. I learned to tap into the wisdom of the Divine with dreams, which I described early in the "Amanda Dream" experience.

I eventually realized that my mind did not have the power to understand what desires or actions were good-for-All. I was realizing more and more the limitations of the mind and the need to rely more on inner wisdom from the Divine. This also helped me realize the material world and its ego illusions were becoming less important, and it was more important to connect with the spiritual worlds and its wisdom. The mind and its powers were of a limited nature.

I realized that this stage of my spiritual development where the power of the mind was primarily used had to take a backseat. Understanding and experiencing the powers and wisdom of the inner spiritual worlds to help with my spiritual unfoldment were much more important than the limited mind had to offer. I also experienced that the power to choose my spiritual destiny increased as I spiritually matured.

Have you ever made a decision where the mind had serious limitations for helping you be a more spiritual person?

Soul-realization

Soul-realization is the recognition that you are the Divine Self in charge of the ego self. This is where Soul's tools can be used for replacing ego habits with spiritual ones. Soul-realization has eight attributes or tools to help you be spiritual.

161

1. **Soul is the conscious observer.** Soul can consciously observe the thoughts and feelings, circumstances of the inner mental and outer world, as well as the divine dimensions. It is aware of what is unproductive in life and has the divine wisdom to know the best spiritual solutions. For example, I had to be aware of my ego complaining habit to be able to know what I needed to change. Since Soul is *awareness,* it is an important spiritual step for replacing ego habits. Soul and not thoughts is the unit of awareness for consciously recognizing reactions and knowing good-for-All solutions and actions.

2. **Soul operates in the Now.** The ego operates in the past and future while Soul operates in the now. The only time that you can be spiritual is in the present moment since that is where the Divine exists and operates. The now is also the only time that we can experience the Divine as well as co-create with it. *Spirituality only has NOW time.*

3. **Soul operates by being.** The ego operates by desiring (i.e., adding something) and fearing (i.e., worry about losing something) while Soul uses "being." As Soul you are already all that you will ever be as a spiritual being, so just simply be what you already are - Soul. Soul co-creates changes in your life by just being what you intend. I didn't want to be a complainer, and had to learn to be divine love to establish it as a new habit. Intentions evolve into the realization that you already are what you want, so just be it. All you have to do is just be divine love by thinking it, feeling it, imagining it, and doing it.

    A helpful technique for "being," is to use affirmations in the present tense. For example, I used the affirmation, "I'm divine love" to replace complaining attitudes and actions. Another affirmation that can be used is, "I'm filled with divine love."

You can also be divine love by going about your daily activities as though you are divine love in action. Co-creative action is doing one thing at a time with total attention to the quality of doing or being it. Divine love and complaining cannot exist at the same time and space, so one will replace the other depending on the focus of your awareness, attention, and actions. Being divine love replaces all ego habits.

4. **Soul is divine love.** Since Soul is of the essence of Divine Energy, which is divine love, the essence of Soul is also divine love. When Soul is in charge, divine love or the good-for-All intention flows through you to co-create divine love in your relationships.

5. **Soul consciously directs attention.** Consciousness is Divine Energy flowing from the Divine Source. Since Soul is pure consciousness too, it has the power to direct your attention consciously by means of your intentions. When consciousness directs your thoughts, feelings, and imagination, it has the power to transform unmanifested energy from the Divine into manifested energy, forms, or situations. Soul's consciousness or awareness has the power to co-create with divine wisdom. The power of consciousness is the power to focus attention, and this in turn affects the unmanifested energy, which attracts the things desired.

6. **Soul is the source of divine wisdom.** Divine Energy and the Divine Self are your sources of divine wisdom for guiding spiritual intentions and actions. When Soul is in charge and you access Divine Stillness, you have access to divine wisdom and its guidance for co-creating what is good-for-All.

7. **Soul is one with the Divine.** Soul is made of the same substance that Divine Energy is. Soul is therefore

163

divine too. You and every other person, no matter how much you are under the influence of the ego, are still divine beings. We are all made of the same Divine Energy. If you strike out to harm anyone, you strike out at the Divine. This is not only the Divine in others, but the Divine that is in you as well. We need to be in a state of oneness with all life, not separate and in conflict with it. Soul lives in unity while the ego exists as a separate form from others. Being Divine, you also have the ability to live in harmony with the purpose and intentions of the Divine Source.

8. **Soul = Soul.** Since all Souls are Divine, we are all equal. Soul is not male or female, old or young, member of a particular race, smart or dumb, gay or straight, Christian or Buddhist, or any other characteristic that makes us different and separate in the ego world. Knowing you are a Divine Self is knowing you are equal to others and they are equal to you. The gender bias toward male domination is changing. The female and male attributes need to be equalized rather than one gender dominating another. As Soul there is no gender. The Divine uses Soul, regardless of gender, to help each other co-create life.

Humans Are Divine Beings Disguised in Ego Rags

Soul-realization is beyond being ego-realized in the process of becoming more spiritual. It increases awareness, power to focus attention, peace, joy, and an increased capacity of divine love to place you in charge of the ego. Be soul-realized.

Inner Peace & Joy Derives from Realizing Yourself as Soul

It wasn't until soul awareness caught my mind complaining at the time of the initial reaction of an ego habit that I eventually gained some real control over it. This happened some 10 years after the ego-realization of my complaining habit. Soul eventually has to be in charge of both the mind and emotions, and its reactions to be more soul-realized.

The reason you have to make a paradigm shift from the ego self to the Divine Self is to take advantage of the tremendous amount of spiritual power Soul has for consciously directing your destiny. Living with Soul in control leads to a personal transformation where you can live in harmony with the divine's plan for peace, justice, security, abundance in the now, joy, and love for all. It has become a necessity rather than an option since humans are massing technological powers that the ego consciousness may use to destroy us. Your decision to transform your identity and be Soul-realized is that important.

The More Soul Controls Your Thoughts;
the More You and the Divine Control Your Destiny

Soul Power Affects Collective Fields

The higher a person's energy vibrates, the greater his or her power will be. Some estimate that the top ten to fifteen percent of the population who have higher spiritual vibrations of love serves to balance out the negative ego energy of the rest of the world. Otherwise, the ego would have already destroyed us. Also, the higher your vibrations are the greater you will serve humanity to change and heighten the consciousness of your own life and that of the Love Age.

165

Are you willing to take one small step a day to increase your spiritual vibrations for the Love Age consciousness?

In groups, love increases in strength by greater than the sum of its parts. This means that the collective consciousness of the sum of the energy vibrations of each person's love will be greater in a group. This collective power is a force that raises the power of people's ability to understand beyond their own personal spiritual consciousness and to have a greater impact on the world's consciousness.

I have found that when I discuss spiritual books in a small group with other spiritual members, it always helps me raise my ability to understand things beyond the level of my own personal awareness. If the group has a negative consciousness, it will have a negative effect. In addition, a community of love helps raise the consciousness of the broader communities that connect with its energy field.

While being in this stage of soul-realization, I learned to hear the outer or inner voice of the Divine. I knew Soul was pure energy and a very powerful co-creator. I also began to realize the divine's plan for myself and others while on Earth.

When I was in this stage, it took a long time to learn, experience, and trust the Divine. People like me who were immersed in the rational mind's consciousness have a difficult time struggling with the ego's mind, trusting the Divine, and letting go of attachments. Intellectual people have a difficult time being spiritual. I feel that I am getting closer and closer to having Soul as the primary self and master of the ego.

The Divine Dwells within Me as the True Me

Do you recognize the Divine dwelling within you as your true self?

166

In no way do I believe that I have completely learned or experienced everything I need to know about Soul-realization. It is a work in progress rather than some final event. I look upon the spiritual-realization stages as a journey or destiny without a finish line.

Currently, I see myself primarily in the Soul-realization and co-realization stages while shifting into Divine-realization. Just remember that these stages of spiritual-realization are mental constructs to provide possible sign posts to make sense of my experiences as well as to help you know more about the possible unfoldment of your spirituality. The stages have relative borders rather than absolute ones.

Co-realization Stage

You probably never heard of the co-realization stage related to spiritual growth. The discussion of co-realization has become more important recently, but its basic concepts have been around for thousands of years. Since there is a major consciousness shift and the need to partner with the Divine, the importance of this stage of spiritual-realization has become crucial for being spiritual.

Our relationship with the Divine is shifting from one where there was a parent/child relationship to a spiritual partnership. Instead of having less power as a child would in the creative process, we have become a partner or co-creator with certain responsibilities. I would think some of you are thinking, Tommy sure hasn't got over his ego habits since he things he's a partner with the Divine.

As the ego consciousness, I wasn't a partner with the Divine in the creative process. I held the illusion that I was the creator or the victim. Mostly, I felt like a child and didn't think I had any creative powers. As Soul or the Divine Self, I have divine qualities and one of them is having freedom of choice and certain responsibilities in the co-creative process. Having the gift of freedom of choice gives me the power to be a partner in co-creating if I choose that relationship. I also have equal responsibilities for helping to bring about the divine's plan for the world.

Co-realization is to understand that each of us is a partner with the Divine and we need to do our part in the co-creative process. It also needs to be understood that the Divine uses other Souls as partners to help materialize our intentions too. For example, you will most likely have a special co-creative or spiritual partner who is significant for this lifetime in helping you to mature spiritually.

If you haven't realized who my spiritual partner is by this time, it is my wife, Audrey. I feel certain that we decided before we were born that we would serve as each other's spiritual partners. When I look back over our life, it is amazing how we arrived together at the point where we are now. She did a lot of pulling and pushing and I did some too.

Since I am going to discuss the co-creative way more extensively in the next book, I am not going to go into any details about how to do it in this book. It is a process of consciously co-creating with the Divine's guidance and other spiritual partners for the good-of-All. By transforming our powers from the ego to Soul by means of co-creating, we will help bring about the Love Age, one Soul at a time. Co-creating combines the most important spiritual power tools we have for changing our lives as well as the worlds. Its three basic tools are: Intend It; Energize It; and Allow It.

This is primarily where I am in my spiritual consciousness. I am now gaining most of my understanding as well as my experiences in the co-realization stage.

Do you see yourself primarily in any of the spiritual-realization stages that were discussed so far?

Divine-realization Stage

Divine-realization is a stage of consciousness that I aspire to reach. I mainly have a mental understanding of what divine-realization is. I have had a few experiences that were glimpses of what it might be like to have this state of consciousness.

The ego-realization and soul-realization stages mainly freed me from the material, mental, and emotional worlds. These worlds are related to the mental and emotional subtle energy bodies or energy fields that surround the physical body. At the level of divine-realization, one is free from reincarnation and karma since lessons were learned. We become free of the memory or Causal subtle bodies where past lifetimes and the current lifetime karma are stored.

Divine-realization is a stage where one becomes a master of all of the spiritual-empowerment tools, love, Divine Stillness, and oneness. I have been placing a lot of attention on experiencing oneness with the Divine by using affirmations and experiencing Divine Stillness in meditation and daily life. This union with the Divine and all life is probably the most important aspect of this stage. It helps us realize the heights of what it means to be spiritual and applying it to our everyday life. At this level, one becomes a master of spirituality, able to serve the Divine to the fullest, and help guide others to these heights of spirituality.

Is it your spiritual intention to be divine-realized?

You're a Spirituality of One

I mentioned earlier about the advertisement of an "Army of One." I never quite understood it since an army's effectiveness rests on large numbers of soldiers obeying orders. Also, an Army is based on a top down structure where soldiers obey their officers. It seemed to be false advertising.

Be Spiritual

When it comes to spirituality, we are truly a spirituality of one. No organization or membership in a religion, no amount of good works, no belief or powerful faith, no reading of a sacred book, no spiritual leader, or anything external to you will give you spirituality. It is something you choose, intend, experience, do, be, and live. It ultimately comes down to you and me making and living spiritual choices. We were given the gift of freedom of choice by the Divine to choose our own spiritual destiny.

The process of spirituality is to use intentions to change yourself and live it rather than trying to change others. You serve as an example of love, peace, and joy that others want to live too. Just be a spirituality of one and by example the world will also want to change to be like you.

Just because you are a spirituality of one, it doesn't mean you are alone. You have a support group that is beyond your imagination especially the ones on the inner. Many people believe in angels or spiritual guides that help them. They are present 24/7 to help you. The love and wisdom of Soul, Divine Energy, and Divine Source are also there to help you. Even on the outer, you have spiritual partners who are here to help you mature spiritually. Others who you might think of as being your enemy are here to help give lessons so you will grow spiritually. There are spiritual giants and spiritual leaders from the past and some living today, which are here to help you on your path of spiritual-realization.

All you have to do is to ask for this help, trust it, and allow your spiritual partners to do their part. Spirituality of one has the best help service desk available, and it's waiting for your intentions, questions, commitment, and doing your part.

The next three chapters will discuss the transition from the Ego Age to the Love Age. This is why being spiritual is so necessary and important for you and the world.

Figure 11.2

SUGGESTED QUESTIONS FOR PERAONAL AND GROUP DISCUSSION

1. Have you experienced any of the spiritual-realization stages?
2. Have you recognized most of your ego habits?
3. Soul has powers for co-creating (awareness, focus attention, and distributing love and wisdom), which one is your best spiritual strength?
4. Have you cancelled out your old life plan and started co-creating a spiritual one?
5. Do you observe your life with objective soul awareness?
6. Have you ever had a feeling of emptiness about life that helped push you forward in you spiritual growth?
7. How do you use divine love or divine wisdom?
8. Have you found discussion groups help you understand more than you would alone?
9. Do you recognize the Divine Self dwelling in you as the true me?
10. Have you committed to being co-realized?
11. Have you ever had an inner experience that gave you guidance about your destiny?
12. Is it your desired spiritual destiny to have divine-realization?
13. Are you a spirituality of one?

☺ *Smile* ☺
You have a tremendous amount of spiritual power.
Be spiritual and it will be yours.

SHIFT V

Ego Age to Love Age

How important is it for you to be spiritual? Is there a major evolutionary change in consciousness happening now? Some believe a major shift from the Ego Age to the Love Age is and will continue to grow, which depends on your commitment to be spiritual. Others believe the world will end in 2012 or sooner. What do you think is happening?

Chapter Twelve

Is 2012 the End or a Shift?

Is 2012 the end of time? Did the ancient Mayans foresee the end of the world or a new age of spirituality? Do you have anything to do with what happens to the world? Will the human consciousness transition from the Ego Age of polarization, conflict, unhappiness, and destruction to the Love Age? These and other questions will be discussed in this chapter.

Since movies, TV, and other media are predicting the destruction or the end of the world in 2012, many are wondering if this will happen. My daughter, BJ, who manages medical clinics, told me that one of the doctors working there asked what she thought about 2012. People are anxious about whether the world will end and if it will happen in 2012.

Some Christians have been hoping for the end of time since the first century AD, which they believe will finally defeat evil. I saw a billboard that read, "The Lord Is Coming – May 11, 2011." I wondered what that was all about and discovered that Harold Camping, a Christian preacher, claimed that the "Rapture" would happen on May 21, 2011, which was to be the end of time. His predictions and others have been happening since Jesus death and the dates come and go without anything happening just as it did on May 21, 2011.

The word "rapture" does not appear anywhere in the Bible. It was instead a religious dogma started during the 17th century where they believed true believing Christians would be taken to Heaven (rapture)in bodily form and nonbelievers would be left behind to fight the evil (Armageddon) at the end of time.

When I was a teenage member of the Methodist church, they didn't discuss much about the end of time or Armageddon. I knew about it, but I thought it was thousands of years in the future. It wasn't until I read Edgar Cayce's predictions about the ocean engulfing the western coast that I became concerned about large scale destruction in America.

Cayce's psychic prediction of destruction in 1958 did not happen. I wrote it off as psychics having difficulty predicting specific dates since they worked on the spiritual dimensions where past and future time doesn't exist. In addition, humans have the freedom of choice and their choices affect what happens in the future, which creates a great deal of uncertainty for those that predict prophecies. Who can predict what humans will choose now or at some time in the future?

The future is highly unpredictable even the Divine does not know what choices we humans will make since we have freedom of choice. The Divine also does not intervene, so we must accept the consequences of our choices. Our cumulative choices are what determine the future and that creates a great deal of uncertainty for those who want to predict it. In addition to Cayce's predictions, I also had my own personal experiences about the possibility of devastating destruction and it poured more energy into my fears.

***

Sometime around 1993 or 1994, I watched a TV program about the time track. The guest led the audience in a time travel exercise and I followed along. I closed my eyes and she told us to select a year in the future to view what we wanted to see. I decided to see the United States in 2025. I believed in the time track, but I didn't think I would ever have an experience seeing a potential future.

Almost instantly, I saw myself high above the United States somewhere over Missouri or Arkansas and looking north. I then looked to the east and everything seemed about the same as it is now. When I looked to the west, I saw the ocean covering the states from California to Washington and on into Colorado or Kansas. I couldn't see exact state boundaries, but it looked like a giant "U" shaped indentation of the ocean covering most of western America. I also saw three or four volcanoes with red-hot lava spewing from them on the northern rim that was probably situated somewhere near Wyoming or Montana. This destruction appeared to have happened sometime before 2025, since Americans were already returned to what seemed normal living.

I then zoomed in closely to a city somewhere in the midwest, which might have been Chicago. There were tall silver skyscrapers towering into the sky that looked something like the Transamerica Building in San Francisco. The people were wearing silver metallic suits that made them look like they might have been from outer space. They looked like us and didn't have to wear breathing apparatus over their head to live in our atmosphere.

When I returned to my daily consciousness, I thought the experience was just something my imagination conjured up. Sometime around 1994 or 1995, my wife was working as a cardiac rehabilitation nurse, and a patient told her about Gordon Michael Scallion's predictions of earth changes. During a later appointment, he gave her a map of Scallion's predictions. When she showed it to me, my mouth dropped about a mile. The western states were submerged under the ocean just as I saw them in my time track experience.

Gordon Michael Scallion's predictions added additional fuel to my fears of devastating earth changes. He predicted they would happen in stages, but his first stage prediction for 1997 didn't happen. I rationalized that it was another psychic having

177

trouble with predicting dates because of the difference of time on the inner and the changing consciousness of humans.

My experiences suggested that there would be widespread destruction but not the end of humans as a species. It made me wonder where was the safest place to live in the U. S.?

***

Many fundamental Christian religions believe in the Armageddon prophecies, which add to this hysteria of destruction. The potential of nations or terrorist using nuclear weapons adds additional fuel to the fear of mass destruction. The more violent climate and earth changes are also adding to this hysteria.

The History Channel TV programs add fuel to the end of the world hysteria. It's trumped up fears are probably good for their ratings, but not for the positive consciousness needed to bring about the Age of Love. On February 15, 2010, I watched a program on the History Channel about the seven potential threats to humans' survival and their order of being the most important potential source for our destruction. They believed the worst threat was climate changes, followed by a pandemics or biological warfare, nuclear war, asteroids hitting Earth, a super volcano exploding, black hole engulfing us, and killer gamma rays from a sunburst. Did you notice that the top three threats were those that are human made and the results of ego choices? We have become our own worst enemy.

> ### The Ego Has Become Our Own Worst Enemy

There is one thing that is a certainty as Charles Schulz pointed out about the end of the world. Fearing that the world will end today is useless since Australia will have already experienced tomorrow.

There is a higher consciousness evolving. World leaders increasingly desire to negotiate conflicts and differences rather than fight. People are protesting in the streets for their freedoms and economic security and there is a concern among world leaders to hold ruthless authoritarian leaders accountable. People are choosing to leave old religions and be more spiritual, to live in tune with the principles of love, and to live in more harmony with others and the environment. These changes are raising the consciousness level here on Earth.

I no longer have to fear being burnt at the stake for my spiritual beliefs. The world has become more tolerant toward other races, women, religions, gays, aged, and ethnic minorities. World circumstances are forcing us to cooperate more on a global level. The world is heading in the right direction through gradual steps, but there are still a lot more steps to take.

During recent massive natural disasters, the compassion of people is flowing much stronger. A day or so after the tornado in Joplin, Missouri occurred; I talked to Bill, a nephew of mine, whose house had been torn to shreds. I was expecting he would feel devastated, but instead he told me how amazed he was that people he didn't even know were doing or offering to do things to help him. He was touched by the love and compassion they were showing. He also told me that right after the tornado he went over to an elderly next door neighbor and others to lend a helping hand. It was interesting that even in times of devastation; the lessons of love are being learned and practiced.

It seems odd, but good is growing because of these mass destructions. This is sometimes how the gifts of love have to be learned by some people. Most of the good in these times of mass destruction we do not see especially since the media loves to find what's negative to air or show on their programs or write in newspapers and magazines.

If this trend of compassion continues, the 2012 fears of total destruction of the human species will have a slim to no chance of materializing. A more positive consciousness has already started to change the ego's tendencies for destruction. The bottom line is that humans must continue to use their conscious intentions to be more spiritual in order to prevent the ego consciousness from destroying the world. Since most of the problems are self-imposed and are consequences of the ego consciousness, I believe the hearts and spirits of humans will co-create a state of harmony with the environment, others, and the Divine.

In *Kryon Book 11*, Lee Carroll wrote that in 1987 Souls decided in the spiritual dimensions that a new energy of peace would prevail. The Armageddon prophesies of the end of the world are therefore not on track to happen anymore depending on our continual choices of being more spiritual. The world was actually on track to end around the turn of the century, but these old prophecies did not materialize since the consciousness of humans has been improving. The question is will it continue to improve?

This, for me, released tons of fears about major destruction happening in the world. If I continued to work in a partnership with the Divine to help increase the spiritual energy vibrations here on Earth, I would not have to fear this destruction. The choice is yours and mine. If we do not continue to raise our own personal consciousness, the transition from the ego to spiritual consciousness will most likely not happen.

While writing my book and reading other's books about the possibility of a new age of spirituality, I gradually realized that by changing my own consciousness, I would help change the world's consciousness. The *Kryon* and Eckhart Tolle books were especially helpful in changing my fears about monumental destruction. They also helped me realize the importance of changing myself to add another changed consciousness for world peace.

You're probably thinking, "Hold on Tommy, just look at all the conflict and violence that is going on in today's world and you would be right. We are in a crucial period of transition between the Ego Era and the Spiritual Era of evolution. I will discuss later that we are in a jump-state of evolution between these two eras. It is true that conflict, protests, and polarization are increasing, which is easy to see and hear since it is in our nation's media on a daily basis. What we do not see is that at the same time people and the world are cooperating and becoming more spiritual. It is therefore the worst of times and the best of times.

Since there are those who are trapped in the ego consciousness and do not want changes, conflict has increased. There will continue to be human conflict, climate changes, volcanoes erupting, and earthquakes like we are experiencing now, but they will be far less destructive than what we would have experienced if the consciousness had not improved. I began to realize, we have the power as co-creators to transform the world into a new Age of Love. My fear of devastating destruction turned into a passion to help transform my ego consciousness to help bring about the Age of Love. I found my purpose for being here on Earth.

Have you found your purpose for being here?

If you allow your consciousness to fear the world ending in 2012, the law of attraction will help draw it to us. Please, place your attention on a world where all of us are co-creators of love and living in a world of peace, joy, and freedom. The Love Age comes about by one changed consciousness at a time or being spiritual.

> ### The Love Age Is Co-created by
> ### One Changed Consciousness at a Time

Will the world be destroyed in 2012 or beyond? It's not likely, but it is still a possibility if enough people do not choose to change their consciousness to be more spiritual and loving.

181

What Is the Importance of 2012?

The Mayan calendar will end on December 21, 2012, which marks the end of the Mayan Great Cycle and the start of another one. On that day, the winter solstice will occur, but it will be a rare one since it has been 26,000 years since the solar system, sun, and our planet were in a rare alignment with the center of our Milky Way galaxy.

John Major Jenkins one of the most well-known independent researchers of the Mayan culture disagrees with those who say the calendar's ending date is a prediction of the end of the world. The anthology, *The Mystery of 2012*, edited by Tami Simon, contains an article by Jenkins called "The Origins of the 2012 Revelation." In his article, he says the Mayans saw "the galactic alignment of era – 2012 as a great opportunity for spiritual seekers to reconnect with the source of perennial wisdom. We shouldn't wait until 2012, for we are in alignment zone now (1980 – 2016). The time, as always, is now." His understanding of the Mayan prediction of a new age was what I have been referring to as the Love Age.

> ### *Mayans Used 2012 as a Beginning of a New Age of Spirituality*

Scientist observed that along with this rare alignment will be some other potential physical Earth changes. Researchers have found the magnetic poles are changing and the strength of the Earth's magnetic pull affects consciousness since it is electrical and magnetic energy too. According to the *Kryon* books, this alignment of the magnetic grid is happening to allow for the increase in energy needed for the new age of spirituality.

It has been theorized that the weaker the magnetic pull, the more consciousness can open to change. Since the west coast of America is one of the weakest magnetic areas, it may be a potential hotbed for change. This could help bring about faster changes in the world's consciousness and help launch the Love Age into a higher gear.

What is the significance of December 21, 2012?

The Mayans established that the date for the ending of the 26,000-year cycle is December 21, 2012. The 2012 date is a Mayan calculation using ancient means to establish when Earth will align with the galaxy and when the old age ends and another begins. I agree with the Mayans that a new age is in process of coming since I have observed changes in my own and other's spiritual consciousness since the 1960s and especially since 1998, but I doubt that the December date of 2012 is the exact date of a new age.

Modern scientific measurements already established the galactic alignment occurred in 1998, which means the alignment has been going on for some time. The Mayans missed it by 14 years out of a 26,000-year cycle without modern instrumentation doesn't seem to be a big deal. Pinpointing an exact date for a 26,000-year cycle really doesn't seem possible, which is according to *Kryon* getting caught up in the problem of earth's linear time structure when in actuality there is only the eternal now. Since we are on clock time here on Earth, deciding that December 21, 2012, is the beginning of the new age can be acceptable to help humans with the need to have beginnings and endings for things.

The year 2012 can become a significant beginning for a shift to a greater spirituality rather than an ending date of our destruction. Hopefully, we continue to improve in spirituality up to December 2012 and beyond. John Major Jenkins believed 2012 was the midpoint of spiritual change in consciousness that would last a century between 1962 and 2062. This may be a more accurate assessment since the 1960s did start a significant change in consciousness. Unfortunately, the baby-boomer generation's desire for a love-based society reversed its priorities and their life styles became a major contributor to the ego consciousness of today's world and its economic problems, conflicts, drug usage, and unhappiness.

Be Spiritual

Should the beginning of the Love Age be set at 1962, 1998, 2012, or some other date? I would prefer to think it started in the 1960s when there were changes in racial and gender equality, "love, not war," non-violence, and other love-oriented states of consciousness that changed people as well as ego institutions. This was the time I personally moved my own consciousness into nonviolence and good-for-other love. This period also initiated a broader search for spirituality that started the merger of Western and Eastern religions. Today, this merger is producing fruit for the consciousness of spirituality. I saw on a church marquee, "God's not looking for spiritual nuts, but for spiritual fruit." I believe this is happening and at a faster pace.

Since there is a great deal of collective consciousness focused on 2012 as a transition date, it would be wise to let it serve as a mid-point for the Love Age, which marks a significant point when the world's spiritual consciousness reaches a higher point. The number of people starting to be more spiritual will most likely significantly increase up to this point and especially beyond. To focus on this intention, I'm proposing that you right now commit to being more spiritual and on December 21, 2012 join with others at conferences or in small groups to "Celebrate the Commitment of Being Spiritual."

In 2012, there will possibly be no noticeable significant event to mark a changed spiritual consciousness since it cannot be seen by the physical eyes except for the behavioral changes it produces. Sensitive spiritual people may feel the heightened vibrations, but most will see nothing or feel any changes taking place. This is why a collective celebration of your commitment and changes would be useful for focusing attention on love and peace at that time.

It is easy to see today's escalation of ego conflicts, but many do not realize it is an ego reaction to the spiritual changes that have occurred. The daily news broadcasts are almost exclusively negative, which keeps attention on the ego consciousness while the positive is hardly noticed. Humanity has to start recognizing the changes in love, freedom, and peace that are going on in the world and become a part of that consciousness. The desires for freedom and peace in Africa and the Middle East have been an example of the increase in conflict and a desire for freedom and a changed consciousness. The protests in America are also indications of this changing consciousness.

The reality of the Love Age can only be in your thoughts, feelings, heart, and imagination and that's how social reality is created. If this is your reality for 2012, it will then be the reality for the Love Age as well. You have the power to determine the meaning of 2012 and beyond by your choices of being spiritual and committing to be a co-creator of love and joining with others in this commitment.

The collective consciousness determines social reality. Since what we think as a collective is what we attract, a focus on December 21, 2012 as a celebration of your commitment to the Love Age will make it so. This date will also be close to the Christmas holidays, which is a time when love and peace has more presence in the hearts of humanity.

Since the beginning of the Love Age is a relative date, you could view it from a personal perspective rather than a collective one. The beginning of the Age of Love could be when you decided to be a spiritual being and make a commitment to co-create love. For me, my change in consciousness started in the early 1960s.

What date would you set as the beginning of your commitment to being spiritual?

I experienced 1998 as a time when a significant movement in my spiritual consciousness happened. In 1998, I started writing this book and made more spiritual progress after that date than I had made during the first 60 years of my life. The galactic alignment most likely helped increase my higher vibrations of spiritual energy that I needed for unfoldment. I believe the effects of the alignment and the increase in energy that significantly increased in 1998 will continue to increase and make it easier for me and you to become more enlightened beings.

185

Have you experienced a change in your spiritual growth since 1998?

Experiencing Higher Energy Vibrations

On the path of tuning into divine presence, oneness, soul awareness, and Divine Stillness, I have periods of strong and weak connections. My spiritual partnership between my wife, myself, and the Divine in the latter months of 2009 and early 2010 went through a rough period.

***

My wife had taken two classes in *Reiki* healing at the University of California, Davis Medical Center and she was enthusiastic about the new direction in her life. I always had an intuitive feeling that she was a healer beyond what she did as a nurse.

In the summer of 2009, she had a past life regression. In her first experience, she was an American Indian boy and she felt free and happy in that lifetime. In the next life experience, it began with an agonizing experience of her feet and legs being on fire and it became so painful that she had to be brought out of the past life regression. She felt it was a past life experience of being burnt at the stake for her healing practices. It put a strong fear in her that it might happen again if she became a healer.

I suspected that this experience changed her enthusiasm about becoming a healer during the fall and winter months of 2009. She didn't do much healing for the family and stopped reading books about it. At times her ego reactions flared up, which tended to drown out her compassionate ways. During these times, it was becoming more difficult to live with her. I had a feeling her Soul had become restless and discontent with the direction her life wasn't taking. She tried to escape by watching TV or being an Internet grandma, but it did nothing for her Soul's inner restlessness.

In February of 2010, she started reading some of her *Reiki* and other spiritual books again. She even decided to attend the Sacramento book discussion group with me. Things were beginning to improve on the home front too. She was getting back to her old compassionate ways.

In March, she decided to take the third level *Reiki* class. I drove her to the *Reiki* master's house where Audrey talked to her about the class. While I was waiting for her to finish, I began to have a high volume of spiritual energy flowing through me. After the meeting, it increased when we went to a store that sold crystals. Crystals were a new interest of Audrey since she had a healing of a blockage in her trachea by a healer using crystals. While Audrey was in the store, she said she felt that the energy there made her feel like she was floating on her feet. She bought some crystals and on our way home, the energy continued to flow through both of us.

I told her that our spiritual partnership was transforming into a higher spiritual level, and she agreed. Later that night, the energy was still flowing, and I couldn't fall asleep. My wife had the same problem. This will often happen when you become a more open channel for Divine Energy until you learn to balance the increased flow of vibrating energy into your body and life.

This increased flow of spirit was like the time lightening hit a tree in my yard, it knocked out the TV and phones. Increased electrical power put our communications out of balance and they didn't work anymore. Lightening is sort of like what an increase in spiritual vibrations will do to your body – put it out of balance. This is the reason small spiritual steps are usually easier to handle than large spiritual jolts of energy vibrations. But I'll take it any way I can get it.

And now for the rest of the increase in spiritual energy power story. My wife has a clock that projects the digital time on the ceiling of the bedroom and the last time I remember seeing it was at 4:30 am. The next morning, we were to attend the Sacramento discussion group and discuss *The Power of Now* book by

Eckhart Tolle at 9:30 in the morning. When it was time to awaken, both of us decided not to attend the meeting. We were too tired. I rolled over and went back to sleep. When I finally awoke that morning, I looked up at the ceiling and saw the time was 11:11. My jaws dropped and I couldn't wait to get up to tell my wife about this seeing-sign.

About four months earlier, I read the book *The Great Shift*, which had some channeled messages of *Kryon* by Lee Carroll. My wife had ordered some more of the *Kryon* books just before she went to the *Reiki* teacher, and I was reading *Kryon Book Eleven, Lifting the Veil* by Lee Carroll. I remembered reading about the significance of seeing the 11:11 time as a sign, but I didn't remember exactly what it meant.

The first thing I did was to turn to the book's index and read the various sections referring to 11:11. The number one represented new beginnings, and the numbers 11:11 represented the *new higher energy* that was helping my wife and I to unfold and bring about a new age of spirituality and peace. The numbers also represented *illumination*. This all related to our current experiences with increased spiritual vibrations. I also thought, this was the symbol that referred to the Love Age, which I had been writing about.

The 11:11 was a seeing-sign to let me know that the increased energy my wife and I were feeling was connected to the spiritual energy of the new age. Sometimes, I wondered if anything was really happening spiritually and this seeing-sign came along to give me additional verification that, yes something indeed was happening.

There was another insight to learn from the 11:11 seeing-sign. In the *Kryon* book, I also read, "It is not a repeated coincidence when you see the 11:11 on your clocks. It is a 'wink' from Spirit to remind you why you are here."

I began to regret my decision about not attending the discussion group that morning. It was my responsibility to be there and to serve as a co-student for sharing spirit's wisdom. The

Love age is not something that will come lightly or without effort. In the *Kryon* books, it mentioned that we may sometimes go to bed tired and awake tired, but it is still our responsibility to help give birth to the new spiritual energy.

This seeing-sign was also a conformation that I was getting help on the inner. The *Kryon* books keep mentioning that in the spiritual worlds we have an inner family of entities that some call angels, inner guides, or spiritual guides that is always with us and helping us. Much of what they do, I have no awareness of. It is also comforting to know that I am not alone in becoming spiritual or helping to bring about the Love Age. Our guides and the Divine work 24/7 to help us do it.

In this chapter, I have discussed the question when the Love Age will happen. I have indicated that it has a higher probability of being a reality than the destruction of the world in 2012. As far as I'm concerned, the Love Age has already started sometime around the early 1960s and 2012 will be a mid-point for a potential significant increase in the shift of this consciousness. As the consciousness changes, there has been an increase in conflict and polarization, which means that we are experiencing a time of conflict as well as a time of increased love.

What happens in 2012 and beyond will be determined by how many of you commit to being spiritual. The future is not set in stone but will be determined by each one of your decisions to be more spiritual. If you are reading this book after 2012, you'll know we are on our way to the Love Age.

The next chapter will focus on placing the Love Age in a broader evolutionary time frame to further provide information about the significance of the time in history we are now living in.

Figure 12.1

SUGGESTED QUESTIONS FOR PERSONAL AND GROUP DISCUSSION

1. Do you believe we are in a transition from an Ego Age to a Love Age?
2. Do you believe the world will be destroyed in 2012 or will it be a transition toward the Love Age?
3. Do you believe we have raised our spiritual awareness high enough so we do not have to go through Armageddon?
4. What small thing have you done today to help humanity transition into the Age of Love?
5. What do you believe is the significance of 2012?
6. Do you believe anything significant will happen on December 21, 2012?
7. Have you experienced a change in your spiritual growth since 1998?
8. Have you ever experienced the 11:11 seeing-sign?
9. Have you decided to be a co-creator of love to help give birth to the Love Age?

☺ *Smile* ☺
Since a new age of love seems more likely,
We will be around for a long time if we choose it

Chapter Thirteen

Evolution of Spiritual Awareness

Humans are now in a period of a potential major evolutionary jump in spiritual awareness that depends on your choices as well as others. If enough people change their consciousness to be spiritual now, the evolutionary jump into the Love Age will increase its likelihood of happening. Again, this depends on you making a personal decision to be a spiritual being of love and living it in your everyday life.

This is not a Pollyanna hope, but has a strong probability of happening if you help choose it. You are living in a time of great significance that greatly depends on your conscious participation in the evolution of awareness from the Ego Era to a Spiritual Era.

Are you becoming more spiritual to increase the likelihood of shifting into the Spiritual Era?

Evolution of Awareness

In this book awareness and consciousness are used interchangeably. When I read in the past about awareness or consciousness, I was confused about what they meant. I always thought of them relating to the state of being conscious or unconscious of life, existence, or the surroundings of my physical environment. Ego is an unconscious state while the Divine Self is a conscious state.

When I was introduced to the concept of a Divine Self, I began to realize it was not only the physical environment I could be aware of, but I could also be aware of inner feelings and thoughts as well as the wisdom, peace, and love of the spiritual dimensions. I also use to think that thoughts were what made me aware, but it's the consciousness of Soul that gives this capacity of awareness to thoughts and to be self-aware. I eventually referred to this as being soul awareness.

When I read *Stillness Speaks* by Eckhart Tolle, he referred to consciousness being forms. He compared it to the forms that water can manifest such as gas, liquid, and ice. I thought to myself that consciousness was also the same as what I referred to as Divine Source, Divine Energy, Divine Self, and all the other subtle body and physical energy forms. Consciousness was the unmanifested energy flowing out of the Divine Source and manifesting into different forms as its vibration rates decreased and eventually became the things we can feel and use here on Earth. Consciousness was not only a state; it was also what gives life to forms.

In Table 13.1 I expanded on Tolle's use of water forms and compare them to broad categories of consciousness forms from unmanifested to physical level manifestations. Remember this is only a comparison to help understand how awareness manifests in different forms like the forms of water can be in different forms. The comparison is not meant to represent an absolute reality, but it can serve as an illustration to understand consciousness as forms.

Table 13.1

COMPARISON OF WATER FORMS
WITH CONSCIOUSNESS FORMS

FORMS OF WATER	FORMS OF CONSCIOUSNESS
Gas	Pure consciousness (Divine Source & Energy)
Steam	Soul's golden energy field
Liquid	Mind and thoughts
Snow	Feelings and imagination
Ice	Physical matter (body)

[Source: Eckhart Tolle, *Stillness Speaks, 2003*]

In essence, you and I as Soul are pure consciousness or awareness. Consciousness existed before birth, during your life-time, and continues to exist after you die. It is who you are as Soul and it is eternal. Consciousness is pure energy that never ceases to exist but only changes its forms. It is a divine gift that gives rise to the world of materiality as well as to who you truly are as a divine being. The powers of awareness also provide the conscious power for co-creating and establish humans as the master of all species with free choice and higher capabilities of awareness.

For a long while, I had no idea that there was an evolution of awareness similar to how the species evolved biologically. It wasn't until I read *The Biology of Belief* book by Bruce H. Lipton, *Spontaneous Evolution* by Lipton and Steve Bhaerman, and *Earth Dance* by Elisabet Sahtouris that this realization unfolded. They discussed the evolution of consciousness mainly from the biological and social perspectives.

Eckhart Tolle's books, *Stillness Speaks, The Power of Now,* and *A New Earth,* added deeper insights into the spiritual level of awareness. Finally, in early 2010 I discovered Lee Carroll's books

Figure 13.1

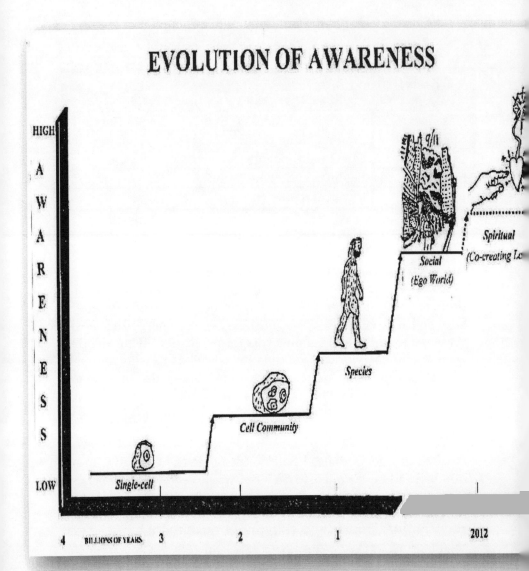

[Sources: Bruce H. Lipton and Steve Bhaerman, *Spontaneous Evolution;* Eckhart Tolle, A *New Earth;* and Lee Carroll's books on *Kryon]*

on *Kryon* that provided additional insights into what was happening with awareness in today's world. I am deeply indebted to these authors for stimulating my thoughts about the evolution of awareness. I added some of my own experiences and observations to theirs to provide an overview of what has or might happen with the evolution of awareness.

Figure 13.1, titled "Evolution of Awareness," depicts the evolutionary eras of biological, social, and a potential spiritual awareness era that evolved over four billion years of life on the planet. I prefer to think of the first three eras as one where physical biological changes primarily affected the increase in awareness. Now, the social era has the primary influence on humans and is based on the ego consciousness. The spiritual era is indicated with dashed lines in Figure 13.1, which humanity may choose as its next evolution of awareness. It has at least started to happen but making it a reality depends on people like you.

The horizontal axis is the timeline for changes in awareness that existed for some four billion years. Do not hold me to the tick marks on the time line that depict the years in billions. They are only relative points in time and probably not that accurate. The break in the timeline indicates how the new changes in awareness are happening at a much faster pace.

The *single-cell, cell community, and species* eras, which I refer to as the biological era took billions of years while the *social era* has been around for only about 100 to 200 thousand years. Scientist now know that biological evolution did not happen by small gradual biological changes, but had long periods of stability and shorter periods of increased conflicts to adjust to a changing environment. This led to a better adjustment to the environment and another long period of relative adjustments. These shorter periods were called jump-start periods or transitions. Evolution of awareness has this same kind of evolutionary pattern. We are now in one of those jump-start periods of transitioning between the ego's Social Era to the Spiritual Era.

195

Be Spiritual

The left-hand or vertical axis of the chart represents the levels or forms of awareness with the lowest level being awareness of the physical world of senses and the highest level being awareness of "pure divine consciousness." These levels of awareness were explained in Table 13.1 that showed the broader forms of consciousness or awareness.

Evolutionary Strategies for Increasing Awareness

During the evolution of life forms, they developed strategies to be more aware of their environments in order to adapt and preserve life. There were three basic strategies. One strategy was to *expand the capability of receiving and sharing information* through biological or consciousness changes. A second strategy was to *increase the specialization* of bodily functions, knowledge, social roles, or spiritual abilities. Finally, the strategy of broadening the scope of one's *community* increased the number contributing to awareness. Table 13.2, Evolution Awareness Strategies, is a summary of these three strategies. I will not explain the strategies in more detail for biological awareness since the focus of the book is on the shift from the social and spiritual eras.

Social Awareness happened when biological solutions could not expand awareness any further and it had to turn to a new source of expanding its community by using the social environment. After increasing the frontal lobe of the brain, the human species increased its power of the mind to use tools or technology, language, and other ways of sharing information between individuals in social groups. This gave birth to the strategy of the social era to *increase the size of social communities* such as families, clans, tribes, towns, cities, states, nations, and now global systems. Species could now pass knowledge from one generation to another through the means of language and its social institutions like the family, education, and religion. This was a strategy for *increasing awareness through teaching the next generation* what the former one learned.

196

Table 13.2
AWARENESS STRATEGIES

STRATEGIES	BIOLOGICAL AWARENESS	SOCIAL AWARENESS	SPIRITUAL AWARENESS
EXPAND CAPABILITY OF RECEIVING & SHARING INFORMATION	Cells increased number of DNA receptors. Instinct awareness.	Expanded frontal lobe of brain increased mental, self-awareness, & language abilities. Social awareness could be passed from one generation to another.	Focused attention on spiritual dimensions and expanded energy vibrations to receive divine wisdom and love. Consciously increased soul awareness to use divine wisdom .
INCREASED SPECIALIZATION	Organs & body systems specialized to increase awareness & body's functions.	Specialized social roles, knowledge, & cultural institutions to increase and pass on awareness.	Specialized in receiving divine wisdom to have good-for-All guidance for co-creating life.
EXPANDED COMMUNITY	Increased number of cells, organs, & bodily systems that cooperated for the good of the total body.	Increased the number in social communities to share knowledge, but ego used conflict to get what was good-for-me.	Broadened community to include spiritual dimensions & cooperated in a spirit of oneness with others, nature, Earth, & Divine for the good-of-All.

[Sources: Bruce H. Lipton and Steve Bhaerman, *Spontaneous Evolution;* Bruce H. Lipton, *The Biology of Belief;* and Elisabet Sahtouris, *Earth Dance*]

Be Spiritual

The expansion of the brain also gave humans the capability of self-awareness where they could view themselves as separate egos from others. Unfortunately, for the ego to protect itself and increase what it received from the environment, it used the *strategy of conflict* that tried to get what's good-for-me. This gave rise to the Ego Era, which also used the strategy of the *specialization of social roles* such as father/mother, teacher/student, CEO/secretary and others to increase specialized awareness or knowledge.

The ego relied on dogmatic thoughts and passed its beliefs and values on to members of its society by means of its religious, political, economic, family, education/science institutions. The conflicting nature of the ego was naturally imbedded in society's institutions, which makes them difficult to change.

The Social Era of the ego is highly affected by conflicts rather than cooperative love, separation rather than unity, war technology rather than being peaceful, greedy abundance for the few, limited rational and faith-based knowing rather than all-encompassing divine wisdom. Since the Ego Era has become so dysfunctional and may annihilate humans and other life, it is now at an evolutionary end-point.

Scientists estimated that of all of the species that have existed since the beginning of life, 99.9% of them are extinct today. If a species doesn't have the awareness to adapt and cooperate at higher levels of wisdom, it most likely will become a member of the extinct club. This should be a wakeup call since the human species' over indulges in conflict and it will not be exempt from a potential extension. That sure sounds like a harsh reality and is a condemnation of the ego consciousness concerning its potential consequences.

In nature and the human body, science has found that cooperation is used so much more than conflict. Unfortunately, humans have reversed the trend with conflict being more dominant. This is the nature of the mental ego. We are currently in a jump-start period between the Social Era and the Spiritual Era, and I hope we learn to do the jumping needed for our consciousness to transition into the next era.

Spiritual Awareness Strategy is our new hope for increasing awareness to resolve the problems that the Ego Era has created. Fortunately, a higher spiritual consciousness is possible now and is starting to gain momentum. The big question is, will you and others continue to choose being spiritual as a new awareness and expand on it? By using the *strategy of expanding awareness into higher communities of spiritual wisdom where love for the good-of-All and a true cooperative spirit of oneness exist,* we will transform into the Spiritual Era where the Age of Love blossoms.

The Spiritual Era is the next possible evolution of awareness. Its basic strategy like previous strategies is to *expand awareness from the communities of cells, organs, and social life to the community of spirit where cooperation for the good-of-All exists.* We will also need to use the strategy of *specialization by taking on the role of being spiritually attuned to a broader spiritual community.* If this happens, humanity will co-create the Love Age where peace, joy, freedom, and harmony with others and the environment abound. It requires the conscious choices and actions of you as a spiritual co-creator to help create this reality.

In the book *Kryon, A New Dispensation, Book 10* by Lee Carroll, he channeled a message about the urgency of creating peace on Earth. Peace is "not only possible, it's probable... to exist is to have peace." In another place, he states, "peace is no longer an option, it is a necessity."

Bruce H. Lipton and Steve Bhaerman believe the cooperative model of communities of cells in our bodies should serve as a model for how the ego evolutionary era should be transformed. There are trillions of cells in your body, which are specialized into organs. They operate in such a high degree of communication, cooperation, unity, and harmony with each other and without your conscious thoughts but still facilitate the body to live in healthy and a vibrant state of balance. They and other biologist such as Elisabet Sahtouris in *Earth Dance,* agree that the cooperative and harmonious nature of the body is an excellent model of how the harmony of love should operate in the social and natural environments.

We are now in a jump-start period where a significant transformation in evolutionary awareness can take place from an ego state to a spiritual state of consciousness. The old ego consciousness in individuals, families, education, religion, economy, and government will be fighting a battle and reacting to any changes that will threaten the consciousness of what is good-for-me. Consequently, conflicts will continue to exist until we transition out of the jump-start period. Most likely, the end of ego conflicts will gradually subside, but the pace depends on how many live in love for the good-of-All.

Pull Out Your Ego Weeds and Harvest a Spiritual You

Some of the changes or shifts in consciousness you will need to make in order to help bring about the Love Age are in Table 13.3. Review them; find out how many shifts you have already made, and the ones you need to make.

When I talk to others about the coming of the Love Age, they immediately complain about the conflicts that exist in today's world; greed of dictators, rich, and corporations; use of war to settle disputes; entrenched beliefs in our ego's social institutions; and the youth who are on drugs and don't want to work. They ask, how can the world be changed when all of this exists?

My answer is that what happens in the world doesn't ultimately depend on anyone except you. You are responsible for yourself and I'm responsible for me. All you need to do is to commit to being the best spiritual person you can be to change your own circumstances, and you will serve as an example of love in action that contributes to world peace and harmony.

Table 13.3
Shifting from the Ego to Spiritual Consciousness

QUES-TIONS	EGO CONSCIOUSNESS	SPIRITUAL CONSCIOUSNESS
What is your relationship with the Divine?	Separation from Divine Secular/atheist Parent/Child Fear-based Faith/dogma-based	Oneness with All Spiritual Partnership Love-based Evidence-based
What is your relationship with other people?	Good-for-me Conflict-based Separation from others Ego protects itself Disharmony Unhappy Victim	Good-for-All Love-based Oneness with others Soul loves itself & others Peace & harmony Joyful Responsible for oneself
How do you communicate with the Divine?	Use secondhand sources Worship & rituals Ego's conditioned habits Mental reasoning	Use direct experiences Divine presence Divine conscious aware-ness Divine Stillness
What are some of the other transitions?	Live in past & future Unconscious choices Passive victim Past karma imprisons Change others & circum-stance Ego habitually reacts Attachment to things	Live in the NOW Conscious intentions Proactive co-creator Free from past karma Change oneself spiritually Use good-for-All inten-tions & actions Detachment from things
Who am I?	Ego self	Divine self

Be Spiritual

Do you believe you are responsible for your own life, which will help us transition into the Love Age?

I am not expecting the end of the species nor fearing it since that would only contribute to attracting it. I see us on track for spiritually making the Love Age a reality.

As I see it, we humans are the Divine's experiments. We were given the freedom of choice as well as advanced mental, emotional, imaginative, language, and dexterity skills. Combine these with having the conscious power of the Divine Self for using intentions and its expanded awareness of what is good-for-All, humans truly seemed to be an experiment for using spiritual awareness for survival. We will consciously have to decide to partner with the Divine to continue our survival or be an extinct species of the 99.9% club .

We can no longer rely on dogmatic scientific models that evolution is based on chance rather than partnering with the Divine. We can no longer rely on religious myths and dogma that God created Earth and life in seven days. Evolution is a reality and we are no longer victims of God's wrath, but responsible for consciously partnering with the Divine to make love work in the world. Our evolution will be what we help to co-create with the Divine.

Do you believe humans will be a successful divine experiment?

The next chapter will examine the significance of you committing to being spiritual. Your conscious participation is greatly needed during this transition period. Realizing you are highly important in making an historic evolutionary jump into the Love Age shows how important and significant you are in today's world.

Are you on board?

Figure 13.4

**SUGGESTED QUESTIONS FOR PERSONAL
AND GROUP DISCUSSION**

1. Do you believe we are in an evolutionary period of jump-starting the Spiritual Era?
2. Is your awareness of pure consciousness growing?
3. Do you use living in the NOW, saying affirmations, verbalizing, visualizing, asking questions, or listening to Divine Stillness to become more spiritually aware?
4. Do you believe the evolution of awareness is transitioning into the Love Age?
5. Do you believe humanity will actually live the consciousness needed for the Age of Love?

☺ *Smile* ☺
*You are in a major evolutionary jump-start period of change,
Are you jumping into a spiritual consciousness filled with
love?*

Chapter Fourteen

Importance of Co-Creating
A Spiritual You

Do you know how important you are? You are a divine being with the co-creative powers of intentions and love that allows you to direct your life consciously for the good-of-All. By living in a partnership with the Divine you have co-creative powers to bring peace and harmony to Earth. You have the power to help co-create the Love Age by just being a loving being in all your personal relationships. Your co-creative choices could very well be the difference between the ego consciousness continuing to increase conflict and unhappiness or even extinction of the human species or having it thrive as a world community of peace and love.

No world leader, athletic star, billionaire, Hollywood star, or spiritual leader is more important than you. As Soul with its power for good, you are equal to all others, and if you use that power, you can be a spiritual pioneer of the Love Age. That's how important you are.

Do you believe you are important for the Love Age?

Your Co-creative Power for Change

There are powers for change more important than sunbursts, magnetic shifts, Mayan predictions, self-help books, nonviolent actions, or other empowerment forces that can affect the reality of the Love Age. This power is as simple as **YOU** deciding to be a loving spiritual being for yourself, family, co-workers, friends, other personal relationships, and the communities where your heart is a member. This personal power to change your life is the greatest *spiritual and co-creative power for peaceful change* in today's world.

> *Spiritualize Your Personal Relationships to*
> *Fill the World with Love*

Your power to affect the transformation of the Love Age lies in your freedom of choice. If you consciously choose to be spiritual, you add more spiritual energy to the collective consciousness, and this helps make the Love Age become more of a reality. As this collective consciousness matures with more Souls joining in, the social evolutionary end-point of the ego consciousness will make a significant jump of spirituality into the Age of Love.

I once thought social change was limited to changing others or social institutions by methods of political change, converting others to my religious dogma, violent revolutions, or nonviolent actions. I have learned that by changing my own consciousness I served as a channel for love, which ultimately helps raise the collective consciousness of groups my energy fields interconnect with.

FROM THE HEARTS OF YOU AND ME

Please ...

May the cool summer breeze of peace flow,
   From deep within the hearts of you and me.

May a jolly baby's laugh echo,
   From deep within the hearts of you and me.

May divine love of the Love Age flow,
   From deep within you and me for all to see.

Albert Einstein said that "The release of atom power has changed everything except our way of thinking, and thus we are being driven unarmed towards a catastrophe." Will Rogers said that "you can't say civilization don't advance, for in every war they kill you a new way." Technological advancements are useful, but unfortunately, most of those in charge of them are of the ego consciousness and use it for wars and greed. The uses of technology need to be guided by those who live for the good-of-All to solve social problems and co-create peace and love.

Divine; Please Change the World and Begin with Me

Good-for-All Protesting

The question is: *What direction will the social evolution of the human ego take?* Will it be for the good of the few who are rich, destruction of all, or the good-for-All? Right now, it is for the few and if this continues, it will be for the good of nobody.

207

This is what the protests and desire for freedom through-out the world are beginning to make authoritarian leaders and good-for-rich economic corporations and institutions realize. People want freedom to choose their destinies and to have the chance for equal opportunity, rather than being subjected to greedy authoritarian leaders and the rich who exist in both capitalists and communist's societies.

The conflict and gap between those who have and those who do not is continuing to increase in this jump-start period we are living in. Change creates conflict and can lead to positive change, so there is nothing innate in conflicts that makes it evil. The key is how a society handles conflicts with either the ego or spiritual consciousness.

The ego consciousness and its revolutions create violence and destruction where the victor controls a new society for its good-of-me benefits. It simply results in one ego controlled government replaced by another ego run leader and group. This is the concern the world has about the Arab Spring where it appears that different ego despots will force their beliefs, authoritarian governments, or religion on others rather than have freedom for the good-of-All.

Hopefully, the protesters will use peacefully practices guided by their spiritual consciousness, divine partnership, and the power of love to reach spiritual solutions for a new society. The Love Age transition will bring more peace and co-create for the good-of-All, rather than line the pockets of a different pro-testing group's desire for their countries' wealthy, religious control, or political power to suppress others. Good-for-All pro-tests are needed to bring freedom, equality, peace, and love to the world.

We will never have good-for-All protesting unless the people who are protesting are increasingly being more spiritual in their own lives. If you're not filled with peace and love, it will be difficult to know how to protest and live in peace and love.

Spirituality is your primary responsibility where you fill yourself with love first to give and live it.

> ### Good-for-All Protesting Helps Co-create Peace & Equality

Are you changing your personal life to help bring about the Age of Love?

The Love Age Commitment

The change needed for the Age of Love is for you to commit to moving beyond your current level of spiritual empowerment by taking small steps to be more spiritual. If you are not ego-realized, it is important to start working on it by recognizing your ego habits, replacing them with spiritual ones, living in divine presence to be guided by its wisdom, and being the divine's co-creative partner. By initiating the spiritual commitment and transforming yourself, you'll help move the Love Age forward. Otherwise, your lack of commitment will make for one less energized Soul, which will make it difficult for the Love Age to happen. Being a co-creator of love starts now and will continue during every present moment of your life.

> ### Time for Co-creating the Love Age Is Now

Are you now committed to being spiritual and replacing ego's habits with new habits of love?

It doesn't matter how many times you tried or committed to being a better spiritual being in the past without having the success you desired. Just use the common sense approach - *"If I mess-up six times, try it seven times and so on."* Since spiritual energy has increased in recent decades, you are living in a time when it will be easier for you to be a more powerful and loving spiritual being.

Be the Best Spiritual Person of Love You Can Be

The shift in consciousness needed for the Love Age depends on you. You cannot wait around and let the destructive ego consciousness continue to gain in power and be increasingly more difficult to change later. The time for change is now. It takes conscious choices and actions on your part to help co-create a better world for yourself and others. The coming changes in consciousness will not be done for you. It requires commitment and help from people like you who are interested enough to read this book and to be spiritual.

Just Be Spiritual and It Will Help Co-create the Age of Love

Are you committed to being spiritual?

You can use the "Spiritual Commitment" on the next page as an affirmation to help energize your spiritual life. It is best to say it aloud in the privacy of your home or out in the peacefulness of nature. You can cut out the copy of this commitment found in Appendix A, sign your name in the blank space, record the date, add additional spiritual commitments if you desire, and hang it on a wall to keep your commitment fresh in mind. Or you can find the "Spiritual Commitment" on the Internet at www.tommyknestrick.com and print a copy for yourself. The commitment will help direct your attention toward being a co-creator with love and energize your intention to materialize it in your personal life.

Spiritual Commitment

I _____
(Say Your Name)
commit to ...

- ☺ *Recognize my ego habits and fears, take responsibility for them, and re-place them.*
- ☺ *Be aware of myself as the Divine Self and a spiritual energy being that's one with All.*
- ☺ *Create peace, joy, and love in all my personal relationships.*
- ☺ *Fill myself with love and giving it to All.*
- ☺ *Receive and use the guidance of divine wisdom.*
- ☺ *Use the power of Soul, mind, feelings, and imagination to co-create good-for-All intentions.*
- ☺ *Intend, energize, and allow what's good-for-All.*
- ☺ *Feel worthy of the Divine's material and spiritual abundance.*
- ☺ *Be one with the Divine and all life.*
- ☺ *Co-create the love Jesus, Buddha, and other enlightened Souls practiced.*
- ☺ *Partner with the Divine and others to co-create the Age of Love.*
- ☺ *Take 30 seconds a day and ask divine wisdom, what small thing can I do today to be spiritual?*

Social Relationships Are a Proving Ground for Spirituality

The social environment and relationships with others have become the main proving grounds for the practice of being spiritual. In Eckhart Tolle's book *The Power of Now*, he has a section titled "Relationships as Spiritual Practice." He uses the relationship between men and women as an example of how the ego "mode of consciousness and all the social, political, and economic structures that it created" has entered "the final stage of collapse."

Are the protest for change throughout the world a sign that this is happening?

When I wrote this current chapter, I was attending the Sacramento book discussion group that met at a local Catholic church, and we discussed Tolle's section on "Relationships as Spiritual Practice." The discussion of how relationships were helping the members made me realize the importance of relationships for spiritual development.

One morning while still in the state of twilight sleep, a state between sleeping and being aware, thoughts poured through my mind from an inner source about how social relationships were proving grounds for spirituality. Relationships serve as a school for testing and learning to be spiritual.

Learning spirituality is done best in families, at work, or in other social relationships rather than secluding yourself in a monastery, ashram, or cave. Life in regular society is where the conditioned mind of the ego is in charge and where you can learn to overcome its dominance. Social relationships are your testing grounds for recognizing ego habits and using the co-creative way to replace them.

Is the ego mind or your spiritual self in charge of your relationships?

***

I saw a church's marquee that said, "We Can Help You Study for Your Final Exam." I thought to myself, there really are no final exams to go to Heaven or be spiritual; there are only daily pop quizzes. Recognizing ego habits and replacing them happens randomly in your daily relationships with others, which are the tests for spirituality.

***

You are now living in the Information Age and it, too, has brought problems. You have accumulated extensive knowledge and can share it quickly even worldwide over the Internet. Unfortunately, this abundance of information can also become overwhelming and distracting. Knowledge is power and can be used either for the greater good or to control others for personal gain.

That is why dictators or greedy rich people of the world want to control what its people can access on public media or the Internet. It is also why political leaders like to control the content of the news and even buy TV and radio stations to broadcast their own propaganda. Those who do not want change are usually the ones using propaganda and fear to control the information people receive. They are not concerned about evidence, since they only communicate what serves their ego's dictates and its greedy desires. This is why America's forefathers were so concerned about the freedom of the press. Democracy needs objective news and evidence-based information to exist for the good-of-All.

The mind and its ego consciousness are poor sources for spiritual guidance, but they are highly useful under the guidance of divine wisdom. When science, reasoning, technology, economy, government, and social relationships are guided by divine wisdom, they will move us into higher, more harmonious, and good-for-All relationships and living.

Do you use divine wisdom to guide your life for the good-of-All?

Operating with soul awareness in control of your life brings the power of love into social relationships. You will leave behind the conflicting behavior of the reactive mind and replace it with what's good-for-All. Putting love into relationships makes the Love Age flourish and thrive. There is no need for worship services since your feet are already in a sacred place where you can live your daily relationships with love and pass its spiritual pop quizzes.

> **Relationships Are Opportunities for Giving and Receiving Love**

Relating to others with divine wisdom and love is proof you have evolved into the spiritual dimensions of love and spirituality. It is a choice you have to make if you want love in yourself and the collective consciousness of your groups.

Are your relationships thriving on divine wisdom and love?

You Are Your Own Master

Being spiritual is being a master of your own destiny by partnering with the Divine. No priest, guru, group, church, or spiritual leaders need stand between you and your spirituality. You have a direct connection with the Divine and its wisdom. This is what you must ultimately rely on.

Others may help you understand, and the Divine often directs you to read books, but you need not rely on a religious organization, author, this book, or spiritual leader for your enlightenment. The potential organization and structure of the Love Age will be much different from that of current religions.

> **"God Has No Religion" – Mahatma Gandhi**

It is already taking place in America where the fastest growing segment are people who belong to no religious group and just call themselves spiritual. They mix and match spiritual beliefs from east and west with their own spiritual experiences to create their own personal spirituality. It is a social movement of spirit in America. In 2008, the Pew Forum on Religion and Public Life researchers placed this group at 16.1% in the United States. In the 18 – 29 age group, the percentage was at 25%. This is an indication that as the youth grow older this trend will continue to increase. I also believe as the Baby-boomer generation retires, more of them will take up their old commitments and become more loving and spiritual. I recently read in an AARP publication that the Baby-boomers are turning to spiritual concerns once they retire. They may give a significant boost to those committed to the Love Age.

The last time I visited Pennsylvania, I heard that the local Methodist church where I attended as a teen and another church in a nearby town where scheduled to be closed. They are not attracting the youth and slowly dying. Catholic religion is decreasing in its membership in the U. S., which is being offset by immigration from Mexico and other countries. These are the changes that are facing organized religion. They will have to change their dogmatic approach to religion and establish a more direct and loving relationship with the Divine if they are to serve the spiritual needs of their people.

Rob, my oldest son, always disliked organized religions. If any of you are like him, you'll find the new spirituality is about as disorganized and individualistic as it comes. Most of the spiritually enlightened will be without any churches or a central organization. There will most likely be loosely organized workshops, retreats, and seminars or conferences given by spiritual leaders. Educational, retreat, and healing centers will probably exist, but there will be no central location or administrative building to organize and guide the Love Age. Small discussion groups that meet in homes to discuss spiritual books or issues along with a diverse selection of spiritual leaders will be the predominate backbone of the Love Age. This was how Christianity originally existed and thrived until organized religious' leaders took over control and banned the *Gnostic* groups and their gospels that practiced a more direct relationship with the Divine.

The Love Age organization will not have a central leadership such as popes, bishops, priests, clergy, rabbis, and ministers. There will be multiple spiritual leaders providing guidance and spiritual people like you following their inner guidance to select what is best for your own spiritual enlightenment guided by good-for-All intentions and actions.

The diversity of beliefs within and without the Love Age groups will require a high degree of tolerance, respect, and love for each other. You will need to pick and choose from available spiritual paths to create your own spirituality. Your path will most likely be one that is lived and applied in every day relationships and guided by direct experiences and love in partnership with the Divine. The reliance on secondhand sources of dogma, rituals, faith, sacred books, symbols, organizations, or a need to evangelize will no longer be needed.

Just don't be attached to your spiritual path or beliefs as though it is the ultimate truth for everyone or try to force it on others as the ego would do. Any path will do as long as it leads you to be the best spiritual being of love you can be. Make it a path of living with love and others will be interested in what you have found and want it for themselves. Spirituality grows by you being an example of it.

There will probably be no worship services, membership fees, or tithing. Spirituality and divine presence will arise out of the daily relationships with families, work, friends, communities, and other social relationships. Your example of love in relationships will serve as advertisement for how to be spiritual.

Spirituality Takes Place Wherever Your Feet Are Located

Sermons We See

Edgar Guest

I'd rather see a sermon than hear one any day;
I'd rather one should walk with me than merely tell the way.

The eye's a better pupil and more willing than the ear,
Fine counsel is confusing, but example's always clear;

And the best of all the preachers are the men who live their creeds,
For to see good put in action is what everybody needs....

[Source: www.sofinesjoyfulmoment.com/quotes/sermon.htm]

The poem "Sermons We See" provides the kind of example of how spreading one's spirituality can be done in the Love Age. Just be a sermon in action. The poem is only a small section of Edgar Guest's poem that I've liked since I read it in college.

The Love Age will not rise out of the ashes of the Ego Age on its own volition. It requires your conscious commitment to be spiritual. If you can't feel or see yourself as a being of love, the Love Age may never happen. The Love Age will be attracted by the power of spiritual intentions. Being a co-creator of love in all your relationships with the Divine and others is the foundation for building a new world and realizing the Age of Love.

If You Want a Changed World, Give It a Spiritual You

The only reason you're not now spiritual is that you do not wholly intend, expect, or commit to being it. You are responsible for your choices and I for mine, which will determine whether the next major era in the evolution of awareness happens. Spirituality is important for your own life's happiness as

217

well as for the divine's plan for the Love Age. If you want a changed world, give the gift of a spiritual you to it. This is how important you are. If you want your life to have purpose, you have to look no further than being spiritual.

Are you willing to allow the Divine to help you make a difference on this planet?

Whatever effort you can do to make it happen will combine with the Divine Energy of others to create a force stronger than you can imagine for peace, love, freedom, and joy. Please, be and do as much as you can to co-create with the Divine to be spiritual.

There is a spiritual principle that if you ask the Divine a question, you will receive an answer. There is also a psychological principle that the best way to change habits or your life is to take small steps. Just take 30 seconds the first thing in the morning or when you have down time like waiting in line for service and ask the Divine.

What small act can I do today to be more spiritual?

Be vigilant for the Divine's answer and at the end of the day record your spiritual action(s) in a journal. If you review it, you will have concrete proof that you are indeed being more spiritual. This in turn will help you to be more motivated to be spiritual. For most it's the small steps that will lead you to spirituality and to master your life. So goes your teeny-tiny steps of being spiritual; so goes the planet's likelihood for the Love Age.

Can you make a 30 second a day commitment to make a better life for yourself and the world?

Figure 14.2

SUGGESTED QUESTIONS FOR PERSONAL AND GROUP DISCUSSION

1. Do you feel you are a pioneer of the Love Age?
2. Do you believe you can affect the collective consciousness by changing your own consciousness?
3. Are you willing to make small progressive changes in your personal relationships to help bring about the Age of Love?
4. Are you going to commit and exert the energy necessary to help shift us into the Love Age?
5. Have you committed yourself to do what is necessary to become spiritual by receiving the Divine guides for doing what's good-of-All?
6. Have you committed yourself to the Spiritual Commitment?
7. When you intend something, do you expect it or visualize being it?
8. Do you allow the Divine to determine the how, when, where, and what that will be co-created with your intentions?
9. Are you committed to replacing ego habits to help bring about the Love Age?
10. Do you use divine wisdom to guide your life for the good-of-All?
11. Are you your own master?
12. Can you handle loosely organized spirituality and tolerate diverse spiritual groups?
15. What is your vision of the Love Age?
16. Are you committed to giving the world the gift of a spiritual you?
17. Are you being the best spiritual you that you can be?

☺ *Smile* ☺
You are of great importance to the Divine and the Love Age.
Are you committed to being spiritual?

Appendix

Commitment Form

Spiritual Commitment

I _____ commit to ...
  (*Write your name*)
Date: _____

☺ *Recognize my ego habits and fears, take responsibility for them, and replace them.*

☺ *Be aware of myself as the Divine Self and a spiritual energy being that's one with All.*

☺ *Co-create peace, joy, and love in all my personal relationships.*

☺ *Fill myself with love and giving it to All.*

☺ *Receive and use the guidance of divine wisdom.*

☺ *Use the power of Soul, mind, feelings, and imagination to co-create good-for-All intentions.*

☺ *Intend, energize, and allow what's good-for-All.*

☺ *Feel worthy of the Divine's material and spiritual abundance.*

☺ *Be one with the Divine and all life.*

☺ *Create the love Jesus, Buddha, and other enlightened Souls practiced.*

☺ *Partner with the Divine and others to co-create the Age of Love.*

☺ _____
  _____

☺ _____
  _____

☺ *Take 30 seconds a day and ask divine wisdom, what small thing can I do today to be spiritual?*

Contact Information

For information about future publications, ordering books, book deals, products, workshops, seminars, conferences, and other Love Age activities, please use www.TommyKnestrick.com.

To order products through the mail you can use the following address:

Love Age Press
P. O. Box 292987
Sacramento, California 95829

Index

O

oneness, 55, 67, 70, 71, 81, 83, 90, 106, 164, 169, 186, 196, 199
other-empowerment, 133, 135, 136, 143, 144, 147, 149, 150, 156
own master, 214

P

paradigm shift, 13, 16, 64, 165
past, vii, 17, 22, 28, 43, 46, 47, 48, 83, 99, 100, 112, 169, 170, 176, 186, 201, 209
past life regression, 46, 186
peace, 1, 16, 17, 22, 32, 61, 67, 72, 74, 75, 76, 83, 87, 109, 128, 133, 135, 145, 146, 147, 148, 149, 151, 160, 164, 165, 170, 180, 181, 184, 185, 188, 199, 205, 207, 211, 218, 223
peaceful, 1, 16, 24, 32, 42, 144, 145, 147, 198, 206, 208
personal relationships, 1, 24, 205, 206, 211, 223
Plato, 63
polarized, 1, 52
polizaration, 70, 89
Popp, Fritz-Albert, 79
psychology, 58, 59, 111

Q

Quakers, vii, 17, 147, 148, 160
quantum levels, 1
Quantum scientists, 1

R

reactive-based, 50
recognized, 1, 16, 35, 39, 87, 151
Reiki energy healing, 78
reincarnation, vii, 17, 169
religion, 1, 27, 28, 30, 45, 49, 55, 59, 140, 144, 145, 170, 197, 200
religions, vii, 1, 13, 20, 30, 33, 42, 44, 49, 83, 85, 87, 156, 178, 179, 184, 214, 215

religious, 1, 29, 30, 32, 49, 58, 62, 102, 142, 145, 146, 149, 150, 198, 206, 208, 214, 215
replaced, 1, 16, 116
responsibile, 16
rituals, 1, 62, 142, 201, 216

S

Science, 1, 79, 80, 81, 144, 160
scientific, 1, 31, 58, 81, 146, 147, 159, 183
secular life, 1
seeing-sign, 188, 189
self-worth, 43, 44, 103, 105, 114, 142
Shadyac, Tom, 1
shifts, 1, 89, 127, 133, 200, 206
Social Era, 195, 198
sociology, 1, 31, 95, 113, 117, 142, 144, 146, 147, 149
Soul, 1, 16 - 24, 56 - 64, 74, 76, 84, 103, 109, 125, 129, 130, 142, 155 - 170, 187, 193, 196, 201, 205, 209, 210, 211, 223
soul awareness, 152
Soul-realization, 1, 158, 161, 164, 167
sound, 21, 74, 83, 116, 118, 128, 141, 160
specialization, 197, 198, 199
spiritual, ii, iii, vii, 1, 13, 16 - 25, 27, 31, 41, 45, 50, 55 - 67, 69 - 81, 83 - 93, 95 - 109, 116, 121 - 133, 135 - 173, 176, 179, 180, 181, 182, 183, 184, 185, 186, 187, 188, 189, 191, 193, 195, 197, 199, 200, 202, 203, 205 - 220, 223
spiritual consciousness, 1, 89, 93, 133, 141, 144, 158, 166, 168, 180, 183, 184, 185, 199
Spiritual Era, 180, 191, 195, 198, 199, 200
spiritual me, 1
spiritual pioneer, 1, 205
spiritual solutions, 1, 13, 162
spiritual tool, 1
spirituality, vii, 1, 62, 70, 76, 90, 126, 130, 133, 136, 138, 142, 144, 169,

170, 175, 180, 182, 183, 184, 188,
206, 212, 213, 214, 215, 216, 217
Spirituality, vii, 1, 125, 128, 133,
143, 169, 170, 182, 212, 216, 217
spiritual-realizations, 1, 156, 158
Spontaneous Evolution, 50, 193, 195
St. Paul, 30, 128
Stillness Speaks, 192, 193
Stranger by the River, 104
subconscious mind, 13, 23, 50
subtle energy fields, 85
synchronicity, 1

T

The Biology of Belief, 50, 73, 193,
196
The Great Shift, 188
The Power of Now, 48, 55, 88, 188,
193, 212
The Subtle Body, 79
thoughts, 1, 18, 21, 22, 42, 44, 46,
50, 73, 74, 80, 98, 99, 101, 109,
112, 117, 118, 162, 163, 185, 193,
195, 198, 199, 212
Tiller, Dr. William, 80
Tolle, Eckhart, 48, 55, 87, 88, 136,
180, 188, 193, 194, 212
Transcendental Meditation, 17
Twitchell, Paul, 104

U

unconscious, 1, 22, 27, 37, 50, 51,
71, 103, 143, 144, 150, 152, 158
unconscious reactions, 1
unity, 67, 70, 71, 81, 89, 90, 106,
164, 198, 199
unmanifested, 20, 21
unmanifested energy, 21, 22, 24, 70,
83, 163

V

vibrations, iii, 1, 21, 60, 74, 83, 85, 87,
88, 89, 133, 136, 165, 166, 180,
184, 185, 196
victimized, 42, 141
visualizations, 1

W

Walsh, Roger, 143
Weiss, Brian L., 46
win/win, vi, 111

Z

Zero Point Field, 79

Made in the USA
Charleston, SC
02 December 2011